The Vagus Nerve

How to Unblock Your Natural Healing Power with Self Help Exercises and Free Yourself from Anxiety, Depression, and Trauma

Kevin Jobson

or indirect, that are incurred as a result of the use of the information contained within this document, including, but not limited to, errors, omissions, or inaccuracies.

Table of Contents

Introduction

What Is the Vagus Nerve?

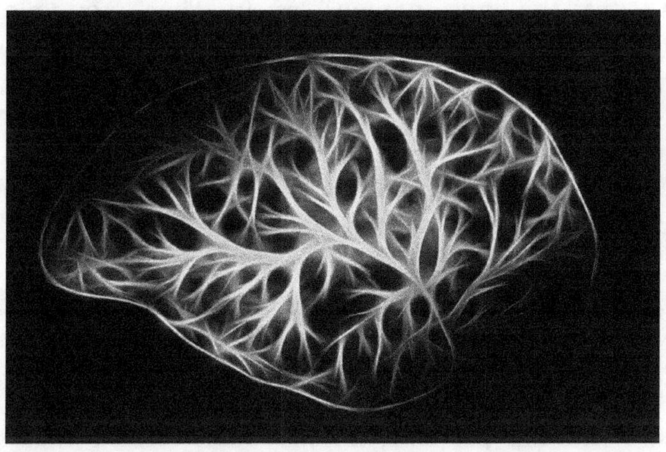

If someone were to tell you that you could improve your mental health by stimulating the vagus nerve, would you know what that meant? Technical jargon and the assumption that everyone with mental health issues is also entirely knowledgeable of the workings of the entire nervous system would mean that the terms are thrown around, without the need for any kind of translation for the layperson. This book aims to put the treatments for and benefits of stimulating the vagus nerve into an easy to follow and understandable format, so that anyone can get help without needing a degree in neurology to interpret it.

In its most literal form, "vagus" is Greek for wanderer. As the longest nerve in the body, the vagus nerve "wanders" from your brain throughout your body. It encompasses the cardiovascular system, the reproductive system, the digestive system, and other organs along the way. So, it's no surprise that a nerve that is responsible for so many basic functions can also be helpful in treating mental health symptoms, for which these other systems can be triggers. Plus, poor mental health can lead to complications within these other systems, as they are all connected by the vagus nerve.

The Autonomic Nervous System

When talking about the vagus nerve, it's good to understand where this nerve fits within the entire nervous system. The Autonomic Nervous System (ANS) is the most important system when thinking of autonomy or actions over which a person has no control, such as sweating or blood pressure regulation. Within the ANS, there are three systems; the Sympathetic Nervous System (SNS), the Parasympathetic Nervous System (PNS), and the Enteric Nervous System (ENS). The vagus nerve provides communication between all of these systems.

The SNS is what creates the body's "fight or flight" response. It raises heart rate, blood pressure, and diverts oxygen from blood to muscles in response to stress or danger. This is done by sending messages using the vagus nerve from the brain to the systems responsible for these responses. When this happens, the nervous system is focussed solely on responding to the danger, so systems such as digestion are put on the back burner until the fight or flight response is deactivated.

To counter this, the PNS works opposite and provides the "rest and digest" response (Chmelik, 2019). This system uses the vagus nerve to send messages to the organs to get them to bring down heart and breathing rates, which calms the body and allows other systems such as digestion to work at full capacity again. To complete the trio of nervous systems, the ENS is responsible for the work of the intestines and also communicates with the Central Nervous System.

When these systems are all working together in harmony, you will have good mental health. All the correct messages will go to the correct systems at the right time via the vagus nerve, so it is vital that this nerve be in good functioning order for these systems to work properly. When the nerve isn't working as it should, conditions such as anxiety, depression, and even arthritis and obesity can take hold.

Superior and Inferior Ganglia

When reading about the vagus nerve, you will likely come across the terms "superior and inferior ganglia." What these are, are groups of neurons or nerve tissue which transmit the senses. They are sometimes called sensory ganglia. The vagus nerve transmits messages from the systems that are contained within it back to the brain, so that issues which may come up can be resolved by speeding up or slowing down various processes. Each of the processes and organs included in the vagus nerve are either part of the superior or inferior ganglia, the inferior being the larger of the two.

Why Has the Vagus Nerve Been Linked to Anxiety, Depression, and Trauma?

When a person is suffering from anxiety and trauma (these two conditions are often interlinked and one can feed into the other), their body activates the fight or flight response within the SNS more often than a neurotypical's brain might do. For example when a person suffering from trauma is triggered, their body goes into fight or flight mode and this can happen many times in a day, or even multiple times in an hour. Similarly, in depressive disorders, the pain a sufferer is feeling can also activate a fight or flight response.

The reason why this is so hard for people is that although the SNS system's function is to help with survival, it is not designed to be active regularly or for long periods of time. The repeated activation of the SNS can have negative side effects such as panic attacks, palpitations, and chest pain. When a person is suffering from such mental health conditions, the PNS will not naturally counteract the SNS activation, which is why these feelings may linger and sufferers can struggle to rid themselves of the feelings of panic and stress.

Communication between the SNS and PNS is facilitated by the vagus nerve; therefore, when communication breaks down and PNS does not kick in, stimulation of the vagus nerve with techniques ranging from electric impulses, to medication, to natural methods such as meditation, can trigger the body to begin using the PNS to calm itself down.

Anxiety and the Vagus Nerve

Anxiety disorders can seriously reduce the quality of a person's life, with panic attacks and other triggering conditions such as IBS making a person somewhat of a slave to their disorder. The feelings of anxiety and panic associated with this disorder happen because of the fight or flight response being triggered more often than it should be as well as when there is no actual danger present. Whenever a person's anxiety is triggered which causes them to panic, the vagus nerve will put the body into a fight or flight mode, which sets off a spiral into anxiety as the body will then be in panic mode which can trigger more anxiety, and so on.

The functions that make anxiety such a difficult condition to live with are all controlled by the vagus nerve, which means that with good training and proper stimulation, the vagus nerve would be key in treating the symptoms in an effort towards curing chronic anxiety.

Depression and the Vagus Nerve

Chronic depressive disorder has been linked to having low vagal tone. This is because the vagus nerve provides vital pathways for all sorts of systems such as the digestive system and the cardiac system. When the vagus nerve isn't functioning at full capacity, the connections between systems don't function as they should, so important messages can get lost or sent with less urgency. This is the reason that anyone who struggles with depression often finds that they don't feel hunger in the same way as they would when they are not experiencing depression, or may routinely experience chronic pain in their chest or stomach.

When the vagus nerve is stimulated, the systems can kick back into life and can improve the quality of life for someone who has been struggling with chronic depression. When these issues are resolved, it will be much easier to start treating the root cause of the depression without the symptoms getting in the way. Vagus nerve stimulation also can treat the root of the depression, as these methods can also bring feelings of positivity.

The Vagus Nerve and Trauma

Living with trauma can be a real struggle due to the lasting effects that it can have on the mind and body. Many people dealing with trauma can suffer from post-traumatic stress disorder, which can incorporate aspects of both anxiety and depression triggered by reminders of what caused their trauma.

Symptoms of PTSD can include a tight chest, stomach issues, and chronic exhaustion; all issues which are controlled in some way by the vagus nerve and therefore, can be helped by the stimulation of the vagus nerve.

Although the symptoms of PTSD and trauma can be treated by stimulating the vagus nerve, the best way to treat the root cause of PTSD is talk therapy for the purpose of dealing with the cause of these feelings. However, if you treat the symptoms and discomfort associated with PTSD by stimulating the vagus nerve first, the task of then tackling the cause of the trauma may feel a little less daunting.

Individual Systems Within the Vagus Nerve

Cardiac

The cardiac branch of the vagus nerve is part of both the superior and inferior ganglia. This system is an important one used for regulating conditions such as anxiety, depression and trauma, as the vagus nerve is responsible for slowing down heart rate. There are sensory nodes within the lungs which detect the speed of our breath. So, when we breath quickly, e.g., when exercising or nervous, the vagus nerve sends information to the brain which sends messages to the heart to speed up and we will feel anxious. Conversely, in terms of calming down when anxious, if deep breathing exercises are utilized, then messages will go to the brain and will be relayed to the heart to slow down, calming the body.

Pulmonary

The pulmonary branch of the vagal nervous system is all about breathing. This section works directly with the cardiac branch, as the lung stretch receptors in the bronchi are activated when a person is breathing deeply and slowly. These receptors send messages along the vagus nerve to the brain, which triggers messages to the cardiac branch to slow the heart rate.

Digestive

The vagus nerve also manages digestion; particularly, the release of digestive enzymes in the stomach, gallbladder, and pancreas. When a person is suffering with anxiety, digestion slows down as the body tries to fight the stress. When the vagus nerve is stimulated as the person calms down, however, this stimulates digestion which can alleviate issues like IBS, commonly found in people with anxiety disorders. Alleviating digestive and stomach issues, which can cause pain and discomfort in turn, creates a positive change in mood, anxiety, and depression.

Esophageal

In the esophageal system, the vagus nerve is responsible for controlling reflexes and involuntary muscles within the esophagus, stomach, gallbladder, pancreas, and small intestine. In terms of its relation to anxiety and the vagus nerve, when a person has anxiety, it can lead to esophageal spasms which are like sudden intense chest pains. This can be controlled with a combination of stress relief methods which will be discussed later in this book. As a person controls their anxiety and stress, the esophageal system will relax and function properly, reducing the spasms and pain.

Vagal Tone

Vagal tone refers to how well an individual responds to stimulation of the vagus nerve. A person in good mental health would have a strong and healthy vagus nerve, so the function of the SNS and PNS would be excellent. High vagal tone is also related to a lower risk of diabetes, cardiovascular disease, and stroke.

Low vagal tone, in contrast, can cause cardiovascular problems and high stress levels, which sometimes contribute to anxiety and other mental health issues. People with chronic anxiety and mental health issues can often have low vagal tone, so their vagus nerve does not function as well as it should, which contributes to a constant lack of PNS response.

A person's vagal tone can be measured by performing an electrocardiogram. If you are concerned that you have a low vagal tone, don't worry! Vagal tone can be raised by a number of activities which will be found in this book, which can lead to an "upward spiral" (Kok & Fredrickson, 2010) or a "feedback loop" wherein increasing vagal tone increases physical and mental health, which in turn, increases vagal tone. So, all is not lost! Note that you can actually inherit low vagal tone (Gottfried, 2017) and in some cases where a pregnant mother has low vagal tone, her child will also be born with low vagal tone.

How This Book Can Help You

This book aims to provide you with all of the tools that you need to increase your own vagal tone and stimulate your vagus nerve, so that you will be able to regulate your own Autonomic Nervous System. All of the methods within this book are all natural and can be done at home. If you are suffering from anxiety, depression or trauma, we hope that the information in this book will help you to take control of your vagus nerve so that you may enjoy living a fully functional, positive life.

If you are looking at pursuing the medical route or have medical conditions outside of anxiety, depression, and trauma, this book will also discuss other uses for the stimulation of the vagus nerve. Surgical and pharmaceutical methods are not the only answer and don't always give the positive effects that you may be expecting. The vagus nerve controls many of the functions within the body and you'll be surprised that, by using a few simple techniques, you can transform the way that your vagus nerve works for you. High vagal tone can transform the way that your body's nervous system works and you will receive both mental and physical benefits.

Chapter 1:

ASMR

What Is ASMR?

You may have heard of ASMR as a term on the internet. It is a relatively fledgling technique of vagus nerve stimulation as compared to the other methods discussed in this book, but its effects are no less effective in treating vagal tone and mental health.

ASMR is a term used to describe sensations caused by audio or visual cues, which can cause a person to "tingle." This tingling sensation runs down from the head and spine which can make the hair on their arms stand on end. Those who experience ASMR find the experience pleasurable and relaxing and much of the time, ASMR is used before bed to relax the watcher/listener for assistance in falling asleep.

ASMR can also be experienced through touch or personal attention, and some people have experienced tingling while visiting an optician or from others running their fingers up and down their arms. However, the way that ASMR has grown to become a community is an example of the way in which people have taken real-life triggers and translated them into videos and audio clips which simulate this personal attention to have readily available.

The content of videos found online can be of almost anything. People have different triggers and things which they enjoy, from eating sounds to simulating getting a massage. It has also been found that if you overuse a trigger, e.g., watch a video of face touching too often, the video or trigger can lose the tingly effect and may no longer work. But triggers and video types can change in effectiveness for a viewer over time and what may work for them one day, may end up not working for them on another day.

The name itself, coined by a woman by the name of Jennifer Allen, was dubbed "autonomous" because it represents a feeling from within, and "sensory" as it stimulates the senses. "Meridian" refers to a peak in the energy pathways of traditional Chinese medicine. "Response" was chosen because it refers to a reaction to a set of stimuli.

Where Did It Come From?

ASMR is a term which was named in 2010. Jennifer Allen first started talking about her experience with the sensation's relaxing qualities through a Facebook group. The tingly feeling or "brain-gasm" (Jamie Lauren Keiles, 2019) had been discussed online for some time, as people had experienced this sensation from everyday activities such as watching puppet shows or having stories read to them. Although plenty of online discussion had occurred, until Allen started her Facebook group, the term ASMR wasn't used.

The group discussed how listening to or watching these types of videos gave them a tingly feeling, which also brought a sense of calm and relaxation. ASMR was discussed for its mental health benefits, as many believers and users listened before sleep to calm their anxious minds, or to distract themselves from feelings of depression or trauma.

It was in this group that the first purpose-made ASMR video was posted; the YouTube video "whisper 1 - hello" by WhisperingLife ASMR. Since then, the movement has grown on YouTube with channels such as ASMR Darling (2.42 million subscribers) and SAS-ASMR (7.84 million subscribers). The community is large and still growing, with ASMR channels putting out in excess of 500 new videos each day, so there is plenty of content on the internet to sink your teeth into.

There is also constant change and development within the genre. What started as people whispering and providing only ASMR audio, now has graduated to full length videos and sub genres. There are real life role-plays, fictional dystopian ASMR, videos that use CGI, videos that are shot on webcam, and more. ASMR cannot be defined as just one thing and the ways in which it helps people are not restricted.

How Does It Relate to the Vagus Nerve?

There is a growing trend within the ASMR community of videos called "cranial nerve examinations." The vagus nerve is a cranial nerve, and in these videos, a doctor will examine the viewers' cranial nerve through a series of tests such as shining a penlight into the eyes and listening to the chest. These videos discuss the cranial nerve system while also triggering an ASMR response. This genre of ASMR videos makes viewers aware of their cranial nerve systems, particularly the vagus nerve, and of an understanding of the vagus nerve and what it does for the body which can help with mindful relaxation techniques. When you know how your brain is functioning, it is easier to find faults and flaws which can be contributing to your mental health issues.

With the "cranial nerve exam" videos and all genres of ASMR videos, the videos are generally used by viewers specifically for the way in which they relax themselves. This is done by stimulating the vagus nerve to trigger a PNS response to calm the viewer. Therefore, even the simulated cranial nerve exam has a real life effect on the nervous system.

One simple way that it works is that many ASMR videos coach their viewers in the mechanics of deep breathing. Whether it be a role-play of a best friend telling you to calm down because they're with you, or a specific breathing focussed video, deep breathing is a trigger which stimulates "lung stretch receptors" (Zimmerman, 2019) which sends information up the vagus nerve to the brain and back down to the heart, telling it to slow the heart rate. This means that deep breathing done by watching ASMR videos has a real effect on the vagus nerve in calming anxiety and panic attacks from trauma, whether a person actually experiences the ASMR tingles or not.

There are also a lot of people who use ASMR as a home remedy for mental health conditions such as anxiety, depression, and trauma. Alongside the general stimulation of the vagus nerve present in all ASMR videos (for those who experience the phenomenon), there are also entire genres dedicated to helping sufferers of mental health conditions. For example, there are therapist role-plays, role-plays of talking with a friend, and videos simulating physical touch. In fact, a 2015 study from the University of Swansea reported that the majority of ASMR users were doing so to self-treat symptoms of anxiety, stress, insomnia, and depression (Pritchard, 2019).

Has ASMR Been Proven to Work?

Studies

As ASMR is a relatively new tool for stimulating the vagus nerve, until recently, very few scientific studies had been done. This phenomenon was only the subject of message boards and Facebook groups until it was taken seriously by the scientific community at large.

A study of those who experience ASMR controlled against a group who do not, at the University of Sheffield, showed positive responses. It was found that while watching ASMR videos, those who experienced ASMR had a greater decrease in heart rate than those who did not (an average decrease of 3.14 beats per minute) (University of Sheffield, 2018).

As it is the vagus nerve stimulating the PNS which triggers a slowing of the heart rate, this shows that experiencing ASMR can lead to a reduction in heart rate and in addition to this, a reduction in the severity of symptoms of anxiety and depression. This is because, as mentioned earlier, stimulating the vagus nerve regularly improves vagal tone, which leads to better mental health and will put participants in an upward spiral. This upward spiral can bring sufferers out of the grasp of chronic mental health conditions like anxiety and depression, and when consistently treated, can keep them at bay forever.

What Do ASMRtists Say?

Although any scientific studies of ASMR are relatively new, ASMR believers and ASMRtists have been raving about the power of the tingle for years. Ever since Jennifer Allen gave a name to the unexplained phenomenon, people have been sharing their experiences, and how it has helped them with sleep, mental health and relaxation. There have been articles, studies, and communities built around the idea that this tingle can be effective in relaxing the body and in effect, treat mental health issues that have plagued people for years.

In fact, as said in The Times (2019), the best evidence for the existence and usefulness of ASMR is the fact that the term exists at all. The reason why ASMR has become so popular is because a community of people who all experienced the same sensation came together online and put words to what was previously only a feeling. Add to this the fact that so many videos are made every day, and that more and more people are online searching for them is the most convincing proof of all.

It has never been quoted as a cure-all solution to mental health, but when used in conjunction with other methods such as medication or therapy, it can be a safe, home remedy to combat anxiety, depression, and trauma symptoms. It can even be used alongside the other methods outlined in this book. Listening to ASMR while treating yourself in other ways can increase the vagal stimulation to work even harder to treat your mental health disorders.

Examples of ASMR

ASMR comes in many forms and the art continues to evolve with the community that creates it. There is very little ASMR which is created by businesses. ASMR is created by the community for the community; and therefore, responds directly to requests and changes from regular viewers. For example, most ASMRtist use ASMR themselves, and therefore make content that appeals to them and triggers their own tingles.

ASMR began with the dark, faceless audio whispering videos but since then as technology and the community has advanced, so has ASMR. If you experience a certain trigger, it is likely there is a video out there to satisfy that "tingle. If not, try requesting your favourite ASMRtist to create a video for you! Most ASMRtists take requests on their YouTube channels, or have patreon pages where for a small fee you can support the artist and have more of a say in what content they put out.

Even though the reach of ASMR genres stretches far and wide, there are specific genres and tropes which ASMRtists come back to time and time again. These are the genres that appeal to the largest audiences or encapsulate a range of triggers, so there is something in there for everyone.

Role-Play

Role-plays are one of the most popular genres within the ASMR community, mainly for their versatility of what kinds of role-plays can be created. Roleplays have become one of the most requested types of video, mainly because the situations that are role-played are actually how viewers found ASMR in the first place. A lot of ASMR viewers talk about first feeling the tingles when in professional situations which included personal attention; for example, visits to the optician, having their makeup done or facials. This personal attention is what a lot of ASMR videos boil down to; those who experience ASMR feel the most tingles when getting one-on-one personal attention and care, which is simulated through these role-play videos.

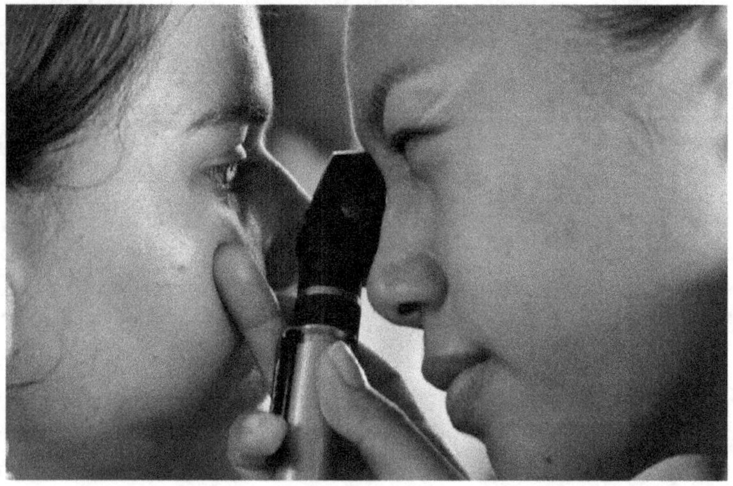

However, there is a world of role-play videos outside of the realm of everyday personal attention. Within ASMR role-play videos, you can find yourself transported to alien planets, living life inside of a commune or even transported back in time. There are subsections of the role-play genre which include being treated like you're a dead body, a piece of art or any other inanimate object! These videos will go to any lengths to help viewers experience tingles and to take their minds off of any mental health issues with which they may be struggling.

This genre has particularly come into its own with the development of technology; particularly, CGI and green screen capabilities. There are videos where CGI robots follow the viewer around to get vital signs aboard a spaceship and where "twins" both care for the viewer and give different levels of personal attention (while actually being one ASMRtist duplicated). This attention to detail when building worlds in which to perform ASMR can work to captivate and and draw in the viewer; therefore, while the ASMR is helping to stimulate the vagus nerve and treat the anxiety, depression and trauma, the fantastical worlds can distract the viewer from any of the troubles that they are having with their mental health.

One question that always comes up when mentioning role-play within the ASMR community is, "Is it sexual?" Those who haven't tried and don't understand ASMR hear the word role-play and immediately jump to the conclusion that this must be sexual, must be some kind of newfangled porn. But that's simply not true. In fact, less than 5% of ASMR viewers use the medium for sexual gratification. ASMR role-plays are non-sexual personal attention sessions, usually consisting of face touching, eye exams, and other non-sexual acts.

Binaural Beats

Binaural beats is the name of a tool that is used across many aspects of anxiety, depression, and trauma treatment, and is sometimes combined with ASMR. Binaural beats are created when two different tones are played, one into each ear, which have a difference in frequency that your brain processes as a beat between the two frequencies. Eventually, your brain synchronises with the differences and hears a beat between the two frequencies in addition to the tones within each ear.

These audio illusion beats have been used for a long time as a stress reliever, for anxiety, and for promoting creativity and positive moods. They are often combined with meditation or yoga to help calm the mind and reduce the thoughts running across the mind, to help focus.

More recently though, binaural beats have been combined with ASMR to create audio illusions that help with tingles and stimulate the vagus nerve; henceforth, aiming to reduce anxiety, depression, and trauma. Particularly when inducing sleep, binaural beats alone can keep the mind awake (although very calm), so this combination with ASMR triggers can help with sleep issues and insomnia, which can be a common problem for those suffering from mental health issues. In a study combining both binaural beats and audio ASMR triggers, it was found that the auditory stimulus from the ASMR triggered the brain to sleep, while the binaural beats kept the brain in a psychologically comfortable state.

ASMRtists have incorporated these binaural beats into their videos as white noise in the back of their role-plays, or just as stand-alone videos. Some people find binaural beats to be an ASMR trigger all on their own, and they only need these tones to trigger their tingles to relax their brains.

Audio Only

As spoken about in the History of ASMR section of this chapter, the first ever ASMR video was an audio-only whisper video. Audio-only ASMR is the oldest genre of video on the internet, but it is still growing and thriving to this day. With audio-only, the ASMRtist invites the listener to use their imagination to fill in the blanks and can transport the listener to far distant lands without the need for fancy technology or effects.

These audio ASMR experiences can come in the form of role-plays; for example, ear cleaning/massage, scalp massage or haircuts. Sometimes they tell stories, like fictional podcasts similar to a series by The Auracle called The Special Powers series. In this series, the listener goes on a journey where they learn about their special powers, meet a new group of people just like them and go on a series of adventures across multiple episodes. These episodes encapsulate different genres of ASMR such as role-play where the listener has an implant fitted and binaural beats, all while only using audio to paint this fictional world.

A great thing about audio-only ASMR is its help in solving problems with insomnia, which is a common symptom for people struggling with anxiety, depression, and trauma. Listening to ASMR audio while you're trying to drop off can relax your mind, can provide a distraction from the anxious thoughts crowding your mind, and is a solution used by many ASMR believers across the internet.

Simple, Satisfying Videos

There is a genre of ASMR videos in existence which are of very low production value, very simple, and quiet. These videos are generally faceless and can be called "satisfying videos." Although this is an ASMR genre, these videos have been known to go viral on other social media without the ASMR tag, as many people who haven't found the community do not know that the tingles they are feeling come from ASMR.

Examples of this genre include cutting soap, squishing slime, and scraping makeup. Usually, these videos involve some kind of cleaning or lines that all match up, as this is the trigger for most viewers. Things which fit together perfectly or can be cut into perfectly equal pieces also fit into this genre. This trigger satisfies viewers because of the "mirror neuron theory," according to Dr. Anita Deak, as the brain reacts as if the viewer is performing this action themself. It's the same reason that we like cakes to be cut into perfectly equal pieces, or pieces of an item to slide perfectly back into its box.

Does This Work for Everyone?

ASMR has always been a phenomenon which disproportionately affects the population. Studies have come up with wildly different results, ranging from 20% to 70% of the population experiencing the tingles. Even so, a lot of people who don't experience ASMR struggle to believe that it's real, as understanding the sensation when you've never felt it is difficult to do.

So, if you try ASMR and it doesn't work for you, don't worry, as there are many more options for you to try to stimulate your vagus nerve, and with the range of ASMR available, perhaps you will just have to try the right trigger and you'll be tingling away. You can actually find "ASMR trigger assortments" or "tingle clinics" on YouTube which are videos specifically designed to help listeners find what tingles best for them by compiling a range of triggers from every genre. This is the best place to start when starting your ASMR journey, as you can quickly and easily find what works for you and then from there, search for new videos with the triggers that tingle best for you.

Chapter 2:

Meditation

What Is Meditation?

When you think of meditation, perhaps monks chanting "OM" in the woods springs to mind. Although this is sometimes the case, meditation involves much more than what you see in films. This practice is both ancient, modern, and mainstream in its form, as it has been used and adapted across a range of communities and its benefits have been passed around for generations.

The Basics

Meditation includes the practice of focusing your brain on one thing for a certain period of time. The ultimate goal of meditation is to clear your mind, but for beginners, it's easiest to focus on one thing and clear your mind of all other clutter. When you first start meditating, you may feel nervous or restless, which is why choosing to focus on one simple thing is best.

For example, to begin, sit down in a quiet place and focus on your breathing. Each time your mind wanders to your worries or things that you have to do later, just bring your thoughts back to your breathing. Focus on making your breaths slower and deeper, thinking about nothing but the in and out of your breath.

A good way to keep your mind focussed on meditation is to listen to a guided meditation via the internet. This is a recording or a live session where someone talks you through the motions of relaxing and meditating, coaching you in slowing your breath, and feeling calm. This means that you can get meditation coaching without having to leave your home, so that you can find your moment of focus and calm from the comfort of your own bedroom. Guided meditations can be found for free across the internet, on apps, websites, and YouTube.

In contrast, there is another type of meditation called *open-monitoring meditation* where you take notice of everything around you. You are to look and notice everything, but not react. This helps you to appreciate the world around you.

There is no wrong way to meditate, as it's all about how you feel and what works for you. The more you meditate, the less time you will spend worrying about doing it "right" and allowing yourself to just be in the moment. In fact, this is one of the few activities where you need next to no skill, and the less time you spend thinking about meditating, the more clear your mind will be and the closer you will get to your desired state.

History

Most people have heard of meditation. It's a practice that has deep roots in religion and spiritualism which has been around for hundreds of thousands of years. Various forms of meditation have existed across many countries such as Tibet and Korea, different cultures, and religions like Buddhism. More recently, meditation has moved into the mainstream, with meditation apps and classes going viral online. This means that meditation is more accessible to a wider audience and more and more people are feeling the calming benefits of clearing their minds.

Some of the earliest recorded reports of meditation can be found as early as 5000 BC in China and Ancient Egypt. At the beginning, meditation was practiced within religions like Sikhism, Judaism, and Buddhism, and was closely tied to these religious practices. It wasn't practiced specifically for wellbeing as it so often is in modern times, although it still had the same benefits. Many people meditated as part of practicing their religion. The practice of meditation began to move across Asia within ancient times, developing and changing within each country and religion. There are examples of this everywhere, from lasuach in Judaism to mentions of meditation in the Vimalakirti Sutra in Buddhism.

Meditation was not practiced in the West until 20 BC, and by this time, it had been popular in Asia for over 4,950 years. This was when Philio of Alexandra wrote about "spiritual exercises," which involved techniques that can be recognised as having a basis in meditation, from concentration and prolonged attention to being "non social." It also appeared in the West in the third century when meditative techniques were developed by Plotinus. However, none of these practices caught on with mass appeal as they had in the rest of the world.

The practice of meditation continued to grow throughout the middle ages across the world, expanding further into the West and Cchristianity. By the eighteenth century, mediation was considered to be a study for intellectuals in the West like Voltaire and Schopenhauer. As travel to Asia and around the world began to increase throughout the eighteenth and nineteenth centuries, meditation began to appear within popular culture in the West, particularly in America. In Chicago in 1893, there was an event called the World Parliament of Religions. It was there that Western audiences in America had their first teachings of meditation from Asian voices with the spiritual roots which started the practice itself. From there, meditation continued to grow in practice in the West.

Although meditation had been around for thousands of years, no real scientific studies were performed on the medical benefits of meditation until the 1960s. B.K. Anand in India found that when Yogis went into a deep meditative trance, they didn't feel sensations, not even when boiling hot test tubes were pressed into their arms. In 1967, a study was presented called The Relaxation Response, which pioneered the benefits of mediation from a biological point of view.

In the present day, meditation is more popular and widespread than ever. Popularised by celebrities such as The Beatles and Mia Farrow in the hippy culture of the 60s and 70s, the demand for meditation services in the West garnered mass appeal. Now you can access meditation through a wide range of channels such as apps, YouTube videos, podcasts, in-person classes, and more. Notably, with the mass appeal comes a demand for a range of types of meditation, so you can try all sorts of secular forms of the art from Buddhist meditation, to Hindu, mindfulness, transcendental, and many more.

How Does It Relate to the Vagus Nerve?

Meditation is a great stimulator of the vagus nerve due to its focus on deep breathing. With meditation, the aim is to clear your mind of clutter and a good way to do this is to focus on lengthening your breath, and thinking only about the in and out of your breath. A key feature of meditation breathing patterns is the low respiration rate with long exhalations, which is ideal for stimulation of the vagus nerve for improving vagal tone.

Deep breathing stimulates the vagus nerve by activating the "lung stretch receptors," which sends impulses up the vagus nerve to the brain. The brain then sends information back down the vagus nerve to the heart, which tells it to slow the heart rate. Lowering the heart rate is the most effective way to relax the body, as it calms the panicky, noxious feelings that can come along with an elevated heart rate.

Vagus nerve stimulation via deep breathing is particularly good for the treatment of mental health conditions like anxiety, depression, and trauma. This is because when stimulating the vagus nerve resulting in a slower heart rate, many of the effects of panic attacks can be reversed. This is indeed good news for sufferers of chronic mental health issues. When a person has a panic attack, their heart rate increases and they struggle to find a way to calm down. When meditating, a person will deepen their breath and the vagus nerve will reduce the heart rate, which can help to bring a person out of the panicky state they're experiencing.

Continued practice of deep breathing will regularly stimulate the vagus nerve which, over time, will also increase vagal tone. Vagal tone is incredibly important for treating mental health disorders because the vagus nerve is responsible for functions that respond to danger to keep you safe. So, when a person is struggling with anxiety, depression, and trauma, their vagus nerve is malfunctioning and telling them that there is danger when there isn't, or is not allowing their body to calm down after a feeling of panic. When the vagal tone is strong, the vagus nerve is functioning perfectly and will allow stress and fear indicators such as high heart rate and redistributing blood flow to key areas to occur only when they are needed by the body, rather than when a person's mental health symptoms are playing up.

So, when you meditate regularly and incorporate this practice into your daily life, you are, in the short term, stimulating your vagus nerve to calm you there and then and in the long term, strengthening your vagal tone so that your body will be better equipped to handle negative mental health symptoms in the future.

Does Meditation Really Work?

As with a lot of natural methods which are championed for their real-life health benefits, there are a lot of people who do notbelieve that regular meditation can have an impact on a person's mental and physical health. However, meditation has been around much longer than anyone can remember and with so many cultures and communities using it, there must be some basis in truth for the effects that believers say they have experienced.

The Studies

The "Breath of Life" study by Roderik J. S. Gerritsen explained how specific respiration styles can affect and tone the vagus nerve. This study proved that meditative styles, both focussed attention and open monitoring, reduce stress markers in heart rate, blood pressure, cortisol levels, and inflammation. These are all stress markers which are controlled by vagus nerve function, so it can be grasped from this that meditation can stimulate the vagus nerve to function better and also improve vagal tone over a longer period of time.

In 2016, a study at Carnegie Mellon University looked into the effects on the vagal tone of candidates who practiced mindful meditation daily. The results indicated a much higher vagal tone by the end of the experiment, with benefits such as higher brain connectivity and function, and lowered inflammation. Both of these are facilitated by the vagus nerve and when these are present, it shows that vagal tone is high. This shows directly how mindful meditation raises vagal tone, and in effect, helps to treat mental health conditions.

Examples of Meditation

Meditation has come a long way in the modern era from being solely the practice of the religious, to becoming a craze that's sweeping the internet. There's a form of mediation available to suit every person, from complete beginners to those who have been practicing for years.

Meditation Across Religion

Meditation has its roots within religion, with Buddhism, Judaism and Sikhism. Those who follow those religions have been practicing the art for thousands of years, but it can be said that all of the main religions, including Islam and Christianity, all perform some kind of meditation in their religious practices.

When most people think of meditation, their minds usually go to India, and for good reason, as India has the widest range and oldest forms of meditation, and a lot of them come from Hinduism. In Hinduism, they practice the eight limbs of yoga: Abstention (Yama), Observance (Niyama), Posture (Asana), Breath Control (Pranayama), Sense Withdrawal (Pratyahara), Concentration (Dharana), Meditation (Dhyanan), and Contemplation (Samadhi). These eight limbs all incorporate forms of meditation within them and yoga is in itself a meditative state, but the Dhyanan branch is particularly dedicated to practicing meditation, which shows how deeply rooted this practice is within Hinduism.

In Buddhism, meditation is integral to the basics of the religion, so much so that it is sometimes thought that meditation is solely a Buddhist practice. Buddhism itself originated from the meditative practices of Siddhartha Gautama, who became enlightened through meditation and became the Buddha. From his original meditative practices, three branches of Buddhism formed, each with their own styles of meditation. There is the Hinayana school which aims to bring enlightenment through meditation, the Vajrayana school which practices esoteric meditation, and Zen Buddhism which practices the koan, where they attempt to solve a puzzle without an answer through meditation.

Another religion that uses meditation within their religious practices is Judaism. Students of the Quabalah use meditation to internalise symbols and absorb the characteristics of these symbols and ideas. The central symbol students aim to internalise and absorb is the tree of life, which encapsulates 11 different aspects of the divine. The individual awakens their higher faculties through the practice of meditation and internalises these symbols so that they can transcend reason.

Within Islam as a whole, meditation isn't practiced widely. However, in the Sufism path of the religion, there is a strong focus on the master-pupil relationship where the master instructs the pupil to perform meditation. This meditation's goal is to keep the heart focussed on God by preventing the mind from wandering. To do this, they use spoken word devices, such as chanting, song, and prayer, invoking God by repeating his holy name.

In Christianity, although meditative processes are used within prayer, the word meditation isn't often used or referenced. The most common occurrences of meditation within the church are followers repeating prayers and observing quiet contemplation, where affirmations and simple ideas are reiterated either out loud or in the mind. There are smaller branches of Christianity, such as the ancient Desert Fathers, who used synchronized breathing patterns and repeated prayer to internalise spiritual truths.

Modern Meditation Variations

As meditation has moved into the mainstream, it has transcended the restrictions of being solely a religious practice, opening the art up to consumption and practice by anyone who wants to focus their mind.

Because of the busy lives that people live nowadays, modern meditation has transformed from a practice of long classes and constant focus to be more like short, consumable bursts. The average modern person is seeking meditation to fit within their busy schedule, so traditional meditation techniques have been combined and converted into short modules that can be consumed quickly and easily. This means that modern consumers can fit in quick meditations on the go, perhaps first thing in the morning before they go to work, or to switch off when they get home.

Plus, because modern meditation has been released from faith and operates entirely apart from the faith-based approach, modern techniques do not include the same rituals and faith teachings as they had previously. Modern meditation has a focus on wellbeing and mental health, and the aim is generally to calm the mind and switch off from the worries and stress of modern life. So, rather than clearing the mind to find space for God or religion, mediation in modern life focuses on calming thoughts to give peace of mind and the space to switch off.

Meditation Apps

A rise in the trends of modern meditation are meditation apps. These apps are all about making the calming power of meditation accessible to anyone with a smartphone.

A good example of a meditation app is Headspace. This app is all about teaching the "why" of the meditation session that you are doing. Before each meditation, you have the option to watch a quick animated video that explains exactly what the meditation is about and how it will benefit you. Headspace is very direct and linear, so you must follow the guided meditations that have been laid out for you and the course is very straightforward and to the point. While using the app, there are a lot of achievements to unlock and goals throughout the course that are designed to hold the user's interest and keep them engaged.

In Calm, another meditation app, the function is a lot more changeable and easier to tailor. There are options to change backgrounds and add in new sounds and background noises which are personally appealing. Calm also gives a lot more variety in the meditations that it offers, as every day, it provides new techniques for you to try and helps you to find the one which works best for you.

YouTube and Podcasts

Another modern way to experience meditation in the modern age is through YouTube. YouTube meditations are free, varied and you can choose from a whole host of meditation styles and teachers. This is a great way to find a meditation to suit you as there is no commitment to any of the meditations you begin, unlike joining a class or buying a subscription to an app or website. If you don't like the style of meditation or teacher, you can just search for a new one! When you do find a style that works for you, you can subscribe to the channel and stay up to date with the newest meditations from your favorite teacher.

Workplace Meditations

A way that meditation has been incorporated into modern life is by adding it into the workday. Companies such as New World Library have added mandatory 10-minute company-wide meditation sessions to each working day, when all employees get together and spend ten minutes following guided meditations, clearing their minds and breathing deeply. It has been found to increase morale and reduce mental health issues within the workplace, and is a great way to begin the working day among the stresses and pressures of modern life.

If you think this is something that would benefit you and your colleagues, why not suggest it in your workplace? Increasing vagal tone across the workforce is something that can only be of benefit, as calm, relaxed employees are generally happier and find work less overwhelming.

Is It for Everyone?

There is no reason that meditation can't be practiced by everyone. The science behind the practice holds up. With its focus on deep breathing and calming the mind, it should have a significant impact on the vagus nerve and therefore, go some ways towards helping with anxiety, depression, and trauma.

However, if you've given meditation a go and find that it isn't working for you in the way you expected, maybe try a new variety. You can find meditations which combine ASMR, yoga, and white noise, and all sorts of other hybrid forms. There's a meditation to suit you and the more you practice clearing your mind and taking those deep breaths, the better you will get at it, and you will feel the effects more strongly and significantly.

Chapter 3:

Massage

What is Massage?

Massage is one of those activities that can be seen as frivolous, the haunt of rich people on holiday, or a sexual act. But massage can be enjoyed in many different ways and when used correctly, can be a solution to many problems that people face in their everyday lives.

The Basics

Massage is administered by kneading, pushing, stretching, and stroking a person's muscles and skin. There are many different techniques and ways of massaging a person, from manually with hands from using massage chairs and massage rollers to manipulation with feet, elbows, and knees. This can also be tailored to the preferences of the massagee, so that you can get anything from a deep tissue massage which uses slow deep strokes and is on the heavier end of the massage spectrum, to light touch massage which uses the fingertips to stimulate energy points and is perfect for those who are sensitive to pain and heavy touch.

Massage treatments can also vary in the products used, as each one has its own specific benefits on top of the massage benefits. The products are generally massage oils with fragrances that promote relaxation and help with reducing friction during the actual massage. As an additional benefit, oils can moisturise the body and scalp. A big part of massage can also be aromatherapy, which is performed using essential oils, candles, and diffusers. These scents are also used to encourage relaxation and stress relief, to allow the massagee to completely lose themself in the healing power of massage.

Other products include salt or sugar scrubs which can exfoliate as the masseuse massages, cold or hot gels to aid in treating muscle pain and injury, specialised body lotions for those with skin conditions such as eczema, and moisturising creams for dry skin issues.

The aim of massage varies from person to person, depending on the needs, wants, and preferences. During a basic massage, a masseuse aims to relax the person who they are massaging, physically trying to knead out the stresses, worries, and knots which can build up within the body. This usually occurs in a spa, but nowadays, you can get a massage in malls, hotels, and from mobile masseuses in the comfort of your own home.

There are also more specific forms of massage which are tailored specifically for the medical conditions that they can help to combat. Massage can be used in the rehabilitation of injuries, treating back pain and stress-related issues such as constipation and high blood pressure.

The History of Massage

The first recorded evidence of massage is before 3000 BC in India, historians believe that massage was present in the Indus Valley Civilisation. Massage was considered by Hindus to be sacred and a source of natural healing, which they called "Ayurveda." Massage therapy was used in the healing of pains, injuries and illnesses much like it is used today. Knowledge of this was passed down through the generations, as its benefits have been reaped for almost 5000 years.

As the world developed and word about the power of massage travelled out of India, it was next recorded in around 2700 BC in China. This is where one of the most renowned early books about massage was written, The Yellow Emperor's Classic Book of Internal

Medicine, which included reference to acupuncture, acupressure, and herbal remedies used in massage.

The art of massage then travelled through much of the ancient world, including references in tomb paintings in Egypt which involved reflexology for the first time and in 1000 BC, coming to Japan and creating what we now know as shiatsu, back then called anma, which was all about stimulating pressure points. Massage also made its way to Ancient Greece and Rome where it was used to condition athletes' bodies before and after sports and was used by Hippocrates to restore health balance. The Roman Baths were also the origin of what we know as spas today, where many Romans got massages to loosen their joints and treat illnesses.

Swedish massage, which is a common technique used in modern day, was developed in the 1800s by Per Henrik Ling and called the Swedish Movement Cure. This technique is all about pressure, stroking, and striking which is used to treat chronic pain. It was further developed in the nineteenth century by Johan George to involve techniques that we would recognise today such as friction and petrissage.

Massage made its way to America in the 1700s in the form of rubbers and medical gymnasts, who used friction and rubbing, and practiced in hospitals to treat orthopedic problems. The first use of the term masseuse or masseur was in the 1800s. They used manipulation of the soft tissue, as we find in today's practices, and also hydrotherapy in their treatments. This was the update from the early Roman bath spas, which were more in keeping with today's spa services and included scrubs and body wraps.

In the 1950s, the American Massage Therapy Association (AMTA) was formed, which brought order and standards to a practice which by this point had been around for almost 5000 years. After this, massage became more holistic, alongside the traditional cures for ailments and injuries. People began to look towards living healthier and stress free lives as modern times became more stressful. This brings us to where massage is today, where there are hundreds of types of massage on the market which can treat and heal a range of issues, or simply help you to unwind after a stressful week.

How Does It Relate to the Vagus Nerve ?

Vagal tone can be improved by stimulating the vagus nerve. Ordinary massage is great for stimulating the vagus nerve as it promotes relaxation and deep breathing. Deep breathing stimulates the vagus nerve by activating the lungs' stretch receptors. This sends messages to the brain that there is no danger; furthermore, the brain sends messages to the heart to slow the heart rate and to tell non essential organs to resume processing.

There are also specific pressure points along the vagus nerve which can be stimulated through massage, which can give a direct link to this nerve and give even better stimulation than regular massages. On the right side of the throat, is the carotid sinus which when massaged, can stimulate the vagus nerve. This technique is used in hospitals to reduce blood pressure, as this sinus supplies the brain with blood and using it to stimulate the vagus nerve can promote relaxation.

There are also vagus nerve reflexes in the feet which, when massaged, can send impulses to the brain and promote relaxation through the lowering of blood pressure and the slowing of heart rate. Thai foot massage focuses directly on these acupressure points, which they call sen lines, and this massage is all about relaxing the body through the stimulation of the sen lines or as we know it, the vagus nerve.

Massage can take control of a system which normally runs autonomously by focussed relaxation and deep breathing. It shows how our bodies can be under our own control when specific focus is paid to the systems that operate within us every day.

Has It Been Proven to Work?

As with many holistic techniques for reducing stress and mental health issues, there are always those who do not believe that a simple technique could have such a profound effect on the body. But as massage has been around for thousands of years, there is plenty of proof that massage can be an effective way to combat anxiety, depression, and trauma.

Studies

There have been studies made about the power of massage in stimulating the vagus nerve as early as in the 1880s. The very first study noted that when massaging the neck and specifically the carotid artery, which is now known as a significant acupressure point for the vagus nerve, seizures were suppressed. By massaging this pressure point, the relaxation response can be triggered in the brain through the stimulation of the vagus nerve, so that blood pressure is lowered and the heart rate is reduced. These two effects of this stimulation can work to reduce seizures and the effect of seizures through relaxation, as stress can be a compelling trigger for seizures.

In a study of labour pain in the Expert Review of Obstetrics and Gynecology, it has been proven that massage can be effective in reducing depression, anxiety, and pain in pregnant women. It has also been shown that when women are in labor, massage can reduce labor pain and actually reduce labor time by and average of 3 hours. The conclusion of these studies is that these functions are controlled in a large part by the vagus nerve; therefore proving that increasing vagal activity by stimulating the nerve through massage can have a big effect on reducing pain, anxiety, and depression. It can also be concluded that if these effects are profound in pregnancy, massage can also have a great effect on non-pregnant sufferers of conditions such as anxiety, depression, and trauma.

A study of massage on the effects of anxiety and depression also showed results that after 12 weeks of regular theraputic massages, there was a mean reduction of 50% in the symptoms of depression and anxiety. It also showed that to keep vagal tone high, massage has to be done regularly as a person may have a regression of symptoms if they stop the therapeutic massage treatments. It showed how vagal tone is a constant journey for any person and demonstrated that therapy must be kept up in order to keep reaping the benefits of high vagal tone.

Other studies have shown that simply touching the skin, the body's largest organ served by the vagus nerve, can also stimulate the vagus nerve. Skin-on-skin contact increases vagal tone and triggers a release of oxytocin and has the effect of lowering blood pressure and heart rate. In fact, the best way to trigger this response is by "firm and not flimsy" touch, much like that which can be found in massage. Just the physical act of firm touch in massage can trigger vagus nerve stimulation and a relaxation and vagal tone increase, which can have such a positive effect on the effects of anxiety, depression, and trauma.

These studies show what believers in the healing power of massage have been saying for thousands of years. Massage in general and specific pressure point massage can trigger the vagus nerve to relax the body through the slowing of the heart rate and the lowering of the blood pressure.

Examples of Massage

Massage is an old and wide-reaching art which can encapsulate a whole range of techniques and ideas, all of which have different effects upon the body and on vagal tone. There are of course many techniques which have been specifically developed to treat the symptoms of anxiety, depression, and trauma. These techniques use ways of stimulating the vagus nerve through massage to promote relaxation, to help alleviate mental health issues.

Ear Massage

An interesting form of massage for vagal stimulation is massaging the ear. In this technique, the ear canal, the concha, and the scalp just behind the ear are massaged. This gentle stimulation and massage is effective in stimulating the vagus nerve and leads to relaxation in most participants. This can be done alone to your own ears or it's possible to get a professional or partner to help you, so that you can completely relax into the process and allow the massage to work its magic on your vagus nerve.

This technique has been adapted and used in ASMR (see previous chapter) and a lot of ASMR videos can be found on YouTube which include ear massage for relaxation. This shows how the sensation or simulated sensation of having your ear massaged triggers an ASMR tingle response, which leads to relaxation and vagal stimulation. This vagal stimulation on a regular basis increases vagal tone which goes a long way towards treating the symptoms of anxiety, depression, and trauma.

Hand Massage

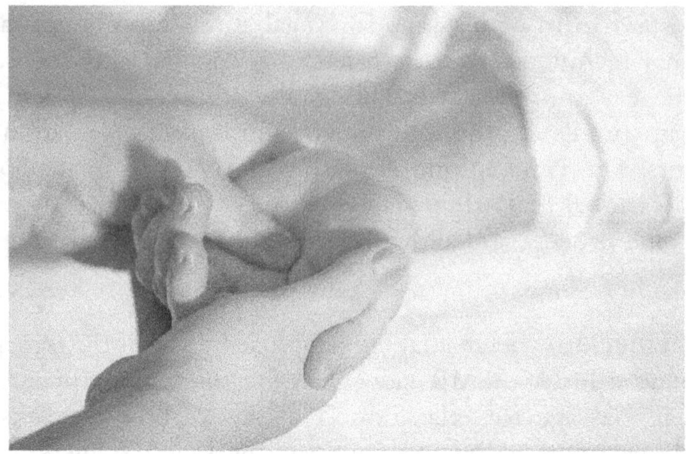

There is a pressure point within the hand which, when massaged, can help to reduce symptoms of anxiety. This pressure point is called the Pericardium 8 which is right in the centre of your palm. This spot is useful for stimulating the vagus nerve as it helps to regulate the major blood vessels that run in and out of your heart, encouraging better blood circulation. This type of massage is therapeutic, as better circulation of blood means that blood pressure can stabilise, which calms the body to treat symptoms of anxiety, depression, and trauma.

This can be done by a professional and this will probably be where you get your best and most effective results. However, if you are suffering with anxiety and find yourself wringing your hands, this could be your body's subconscious way of directing you towards this pressure point and self-massage may alleviate the anxiety symptoms that you are feeling.

Chinese Self-Massage

In Chinese medicine, acupressure points have been used as a form of healing for thousands of years. The idea behind this is that everyone has lines called meridians which are invisible channels which run across the body, and when these lines are stimulated by pressure, blockages in your Meridians can be removed to cure discomfort, pain, and illness.

How does this relate to the vagus nerve? Well, the meridians found in acupressure can line up with the vagus nerve, and when this happens and the correct acupressure point on the vagus nerve is stimulated, it can send messages down the vagus nerve telling the body to relax. The whole act of massaging acupressure points on the body is completely focussed on relieving anxiety and calming the body, so when a person starts breathing deeply as mentioned previously, lung stretch receptors are activated leading to a chain reaction of heart rate decreasing and digestive function increasing, allowing a person to calm down. This can help a lot when repeated over a long period of time, as it will have the effect of increasing vagal tone, which has a positive effect on mental illness.

This acupressure massage can be done at home when you learn the points and practice pressing on them, but there are other ways of stimulating acupoints. One example is acupuncture. Acupuncture would not be recommended to be performed by anyone other than a professional as it is a very extreme form of massage for reducing anxiety through vagal stimulation. It involves sticking very thin, very sharp needles through acupressure points, which like massage, can remove blockages in the meridians and reduce anxiety, depression, and trauma.

Hot Stone Massage

Another technique that adds pressure to specific pressure points on the body is hot stone massage. In this type of massage, the masseuse will apply hot, smooth stones to specific areas of the body, where the pressure and stimulation of the hot stone will affect the body (and vagus nerve in the correct locations) which promotes relaxation. This relaxation will further stimulate the vagus nerve as the stretch receptors in the lung are activated and the body will reduce its heart rate. Regular massage in this way will increase vagal tone, and doing so can treat and prevent mental health issues such as anxiety, depression and trauma.

Other At-Home Massage Techniques

You can simulate many different types of massages just by using your own hands. As mentioned earlier in this chapter, the easiest and most effective way to massage yourself for vagus nerve stimulation is by massaging the carotid artery along the neck and also massaging the feet. These techniques have been used to encourage infant weight gain as they stimulate the vagus nerve to relax the body and when the body is relaxed, it allows for proper digestive function and absorption of nutrients.

There is also lots of equipment that you can buy online which can assist with at-home massages. For example, you can buy heavy-duty massage guns which simulate deep tissue massages by burrowing deep into the muscle and undoing all of the knots that have built up. There are also other less intense forms of tools made for undoing knots, such as massage rollers. These can be used for massaging areas such as the carotid arteries which will stimulate the vagus nerve and lead to relaxation, and over time, increase overall vagal tone for mental health.

There are a range of massage chairs and pillows available which can target specific areas, and simulate specific types of massage. There are Shiatsu massage pillows which apply heat and pressure to your back (or wherever you place the pillow) which promote relaxation, deep breathing, and vagal stimulation. There are also specific neck massagers, which could be used for applying pressure to the carotid arteries for vagal stimulation.

Another massage that can be tried at home is acupressure. There is a growing trend in acupressure mats, which have lots of plastic spikes which you lie on and it stimulates the acupressure points along your meridian lines. These range from very sharp to softer spikes depending on your tolerance and you can also change your clothing to fit how much pressure you want. For example, bare skin would be the sharpest feeling and you can wear different thicknesses of tshirt for a softer effect. It has been speculated that the pain results in a parasympathetic response and that the vagal stimulation leads to relaxation and some relief from the symptoms of anxiety, depression, and trauma.

Is Massage a Treatment for Everyone?

Although massage has had positive effects on the majority of those who have experienced it and used it to treat their mental health symptoms, there are always people for whom this technique does not work. In some studies where the consensus is generally positive that the experience has improved anxiety, depression, and trauma in participants, in some cases, there are outliers for whom the treatment actually triggered panic attacks and a worsening of symptoms.

For sufferers who are sensitive to touch, or can be triggered by the touch of strangers, this may be the case. However, repeated exposure to touch could potentially achieve a desensitization to these triggers and generally improve quality of life. Like all holistic methods, massage can take time to show lasting effects. Although you will feel the benefits from your first session, if you keep up with the treatment and find the method which works best for you, you will reap the benefits in the long term of higher vagal tone and relief from the symptoms of anxiety, depression, and trauma.

Chapter 4:

Cold Water Therapy

If we're talking about natural, holistic methods of treating mental health issues such as anxiety, depression, and trauma, there's nothing more natural than cold water. This is a technique that anyone can try at no cost to themselves, with methods ranging from a shower at home to swimming the English channel.

What Is the Cold Water Technique?

You might be wondering why you would want to switch out steamy hot showers for an ice cold blast, but this section will explain the healing benefits of exposing your body to ice cold water. It's a technique which has been used for thousands of years, but the reasons behind the myriad of benefits have only been discovered recently.

The Basics

Have you ever felt anxious or depressed to the point where you felt as though you were moving through a fog? If you have, I bet you've splashed cold water on your face as a way of waking yourself up or snapping yourself out of it. Cold water bathing and the general use of cold water has been around for a long time and can be used to treat a whole range of ailments and symptoms.

One place that the power of cold water is harnessed is in the beauty world. For years, hairdressers have been telling their clients to give their hair a rinse with cold water at the end of their shower. This technique locks moisture inside of the hair cuticle and gives shinier hair for longer. Another beauty tip for using cold water is using it to wash your face, as the cold water tightens pores and makes them less visible. This also seals your skin and prevents bacteria from entering your pores, which can stop acne and spots from forming under the skin.

Another unexpected benefit of bathing in cold water is that, if you take a cold shower once a day, you can lose up to 9 pounds in a year. The cold water stimulates brown fat and provides lymphatic drainage, which assists in the weight loss process. So, cold water alone and its effects may not be noticeable for a while, but if you include cold showers in your weight loss routine, they could increase your overall weight loss and help you to achieve your goals.

History

Cold water therapy has been used since ancient times. The first recorded accounts of cold water swimming are found with the ancient Greeks, who celebrated cold water diving or "wild swimming" through places such as the fresco at the tomb of the diver. Cold water has been used throughout history through necessity, as hot water taps did not exist; all bathing and cleaning was done in cold water, whether in lakes and rivers or in actual baths.

In the eighteenth century, the book *On the Healing Virtues of Cold Water, Inwardly and Outwardly Applied* by Dr. Hahn was written. This was when baths began to be medically prescribed for all manner of ailments from pain to hysteria. However, even Hippocrates had prescribed cold water bathing to "allay latitude" or to get rid of physical or mental weariness. So, the healing properties of cold water bathing and its use have been well recorded throughout history.

Cold water bathing reached a peak in its craze in the UK in the Victorian era, when well-known names such as Florence Nightingale, Thomas Carlyle, and Charles Darwin all went for treatment at a clinic in Malvern. The old Roman baths were used and people came from far and wide to treat their illnesses and pain.

To this day, people still use the power of cold water and cold water bathing for a host of reasons, from skincare to weight loss. Sometimes the simplest cures are the most effective ones and people throughout history have been raving about this one for centuries.

How Does It Relate to the Vagus Nerve?

Cold water therapy works by activating the body's response to temperature changes. This is the same response as the fight or flight response, which is the body's natural response to perceived danger. The danger in this case simulates falling into freezing water or being in freezing temperatures which are not conducive to the body's natural function.

When the body is exposed to freezing water, sensors on the vagus nerve send messages to the brain to activate the fight or flight response. This then triggers the brain to send more messages back down the vagus nerve to divert blood away from less vital processes such as the digestive system, and sends them to the heart. This increases the heart rate, breathing quickens, and the body is flooded with adrenaline. All of this occurs naturally in order to trigger the body to panic in response to the perceived danger, so that the body can work harder in the short term to combat the danger.

Cold water therapy harnesses the fight or flight response by slowly desensitising the body. In the short term, this therapy works by shocking the body into a fight or flight mode, and then giving relief when the water is removed as your body relaxes. The vagus nerve will then sense that the body is out of danger and will turn off the fight or flight response, and normal function will return to the body, including the normalization of the heart rate and blood pressure. This can alleviate symptoms of anxiety as the relief from coming out of the cold water can deactivate the fight or flight response that originated from both the water and the anxiety.

In the long term, repeated exposure to cold water therapy can teach your body to acclimate to the feelings of stress. When you regularly bathe in cold water, your body gets used to the feeling of panic and is less likely to activate the fight or flight response to the same extreme. With increased practice, you will be able to spend more and more time in the water as your body gets used to it. A good way to train your body to reduce the fight or flight response is to combine cold water therapy with meditation. If you focus your mind on breathing while you sit in the cold water, you can teach your body to relax in stressful conditions to delay the fight or flight response . The benefits are transferable as treatment for the symptoms of anxiety, depression, and trauma, as they are affected by the same fight or flight response. Training your body to reduce its reaction time and to relax under stress can also reduce the symptoms of mental health disorders over time.

Cold water therapy also triggers the vagus nerve, which exercises it. In particular, repeated exposure can increase vagal tone. High vagal tone is synonymous with strong mental health and when a person increases their vagal tone, they are also reducing their susceptibility to mental health disorders such as anxiety, depression, and trauma.

Has It been Proven to Work?

Studies

There have been many studies of the impact of exposure to cold water therapy on the vagus nerve and the body in general. This natural, holistic method of treating mental health problems has been used for thousands of years and has always been revered for its uses in treating illnesses and ailments. But, as we've come into modern times, studies have been made to determine why this impact occurs and prove that this treatment really works. Scientists want to know for sure that results are not just a placebo effect, but that this therapy truly does have an effect in combating anxiety, depression, and trauma.

In a study by the Institute for Health and Behaviour in Luxemburg, participants were treated with cold water stimulation on their left cheeks, necks, and forearms. This was tested for its effect on heart rate during the stimulation, both for its variability and reduction in rate. The study showed that, when stimulated with cold water, heart rate variability increased and heart rate decreased. This is important for the treatment of mental health through vagus nerve stimulation, as the increase in heart rate activity occurs because the vagus nerve is stimulated to make this happen. This means that vagal tone is improved every time that cold water therapy is used, which is an important factor in treating the long term effects of chronic mental health issues. This study also showed that the neck was the most effective location in terms of vagal activity, which makes sense because it's the location of the carotid artery, which is directly linked to the vagus nerve and when stimulated, can have positive effects on relaxing the body and treating mental health.

In another study done in Germany, the bodies of cold water swimmers were evaluated before and after cold winter swimming in outdoor conditions. The study showed that repeated exposure to the cold water stimulus led to a decrease in the uric acid concentration of the body.

How is that important? Well, reduced uric acid in the body can lead to body hardening, which increases a person's tolerance for stress and other diseases. This relates to the vagus nerve as this mechanism for reducing uric acid concentration comes from stimulation of the vagus nerve with cold water exposure. In whole, repeated vagal stimulation increases vagal tone, showing real positive effects in reducing stress and the effects of mental health disorders.

Cold water therapy has been studied specifically for its positive effects in treating depression. In a study by Nikolai A. Shevchuk, the effect of daily cold showers with lengths of shower increasing daily over several months was studied for its effects on people suffering with depression. It was found that the parasympathetic nervous system was activated by vagal stimulation from the cold water, which sent messages to the brain to release beta-endorphin and noradrenaline which worked to combat depression. The massive increase in electrical impulses being sent down the vagus nerve during the cold shower also has been hypothesised to have an antidepressant effect, as it stimulates the fight or flight response which is entirely the opposite of feeling lethargic and unable to move. This study was a big success and showed how regular cold water therapy can be key in treating depression using natural, holistic methods.

These studies clearly show a correlation between the use of cold water therapy, whether it be cold showers or specific hydrotherapy, and the reduction in the symptoms of mental health disorders. In fact, there have even been studies by Dubois in 2010 which showed that, when compared with drug therapy for anxiety, cold water therapy actually showed more positive results in reducing the effects of the disorder. So, even though you will find non-believers in the effects of natural, holistic methods, science has shown that these treatments truly do work and can be even more effective than drug therapy.

What Else Can It Help With?

Cold water is not only a great solution for mental health issues, it also can have an effect on other illnesses and ailments through the stimulation of the vagus nerve. Inflammation is one of the conditions that can be combated with cold water therapy. When a body part is inflamed or swollen, one of the best cures is to hold it under cold water for some time. So, it makes sense that repeated cold water therapy can reduce inflammation over a longer period of time.

Many conditions can also be associated with inflammation and therefore treating the inflammation with cold water therapy can also have a positive impact on treating those conditions as well. For example, autoimmune diseases come from chronic inflammation within the body, so treating the inflammation can reduce or even cure some autoimmune diseases to improve quality of life. Other conditions that can be treated include arthritis and joint pain, all of which improve when cold water therapy is used to combat the root cause of the inflammation.

Inflammation is also associated with anxiety and depression, so on top of the vagal tone improvements helping with mental health issues, reducing the inflammation through cold water therapy works twofold to combat the symptoms of anxiety, depression, and trauma.

Examples and Variations of Cold Water Therapy

Cold water therapy can be applied in many ways and forms, all of which use the same basic technique of shocking the body into creating a parasympathetic response.

Cold Showers

One of the easiest methods of cold water therapy to apply to anyone's morning routine is taking a cold shower. This can be incorporated by either taking a completely cold shower, or by ending an ordinary shower by blasting as much cold water as you can take. This can be upped every day as tolerance increases and the longer the shower, the more stimulation of the vagus nerve will occur and the greater the effects of cold water therapy will be felt.

A morning cold shower is also seen as a great way to wake your body and brain up, shocking yourself awake and giving you a great base from which to start the day. This can make you more alert and reduce the mind-clouding effects of anxiety and depression, so that you can feel more present and ready to take on all of the things that you need to do during the day.

Both cold showers and ending a shower with a cold rinse have been championed by hairstylists for years. Not only do they have a positive effect on anxiety, depression, and trauma by parasympathetic response, but the hair also benefits from this practice, as the hair cuticle becomes closed, trapping moisture inside for shinier and more gorgeous locks. So, it's a double whammy; you can find some relief from the mental health issues that you're struggling with while also improving your hair's texture and quality.

Cold Water Immersion

Cold ice baths are a treatment that have been used by athletes for years as a way to recover from the discomfort sometimes caused by extreme exercise and muscle use. This treatment reduces muscle soreness by stimulating the vagus nerve to reduce inflammation and constrict blood vessels, which in turn, reduces blood flow to the overworked muscles. The reduced blood flow combats the feeling of soreness, which means that recovery from exercise is made much easier and less painful.

If it's good enough for extreme athletes, then it's good enough to help to treat your mental health. Cold baths have all the best effects of cold water therapy, with the strong vagal stimulation leading to a reduction in heart rate and the calming effect on the body. In addition, regular stimulation of the vagus nerve in this way will increase vagal tone to reduce the effects of chronic depression, anxiety, and trauma.

Another great thing about taking cold baths is that they are a perfect way to incorporate another vagus nerve stimulation technique to make the most of these anxiety and depression beating treatments, that being the practice of meditation. A cold bath is the perfect place to practice meditation techniques. The focus on deep breathing will work in two ways; by stimulating the vagus nerve to calm the body, as well as by helping the body to accept sudden temperature change. As discussed in the earlier chapter, meditation relaxes the body by reducing the fight or flight response, also reducing the panic that can occur when the body is exposed to extreme temperature conditions. This can mean that a cold bath will be a more pleasant experience while also increasing the vagal stimulation at the same time, giving twice the anxiety and depression beating effects.

Open Water Swimming

A natural method of exposing your body to cold water therapy is open water swimming or wild swimming. Open water swimming has been around for thousands of years, initially as a method of bathing back in ancient times, and later as a method of pushing oneself to try swimming in more difficult and colder conditions. Wild swimming makes the whole world your swimming bath and variations can take place in lakes, rivers, outdoor pools or lidos, and even in the sea. This can be done alone or in groups and there are teams of people who will come together to celebrate the feeling of swimming wild and free in natural water formations. More extreme forms of this can be seen where people take on challenges such as swimming the English Channel, which can push their bodies to the absolute limits of their capabilities.

Wild swimming is a great method of cold water therapy, as it applies all of the vagus nerve stimulating effects while also pushing a body to do something athletic and productive. This can be an effective distraction from the issues of anxiety, depression, and trauma, as it will take the mind off of triggers for panic attacks and depressive states.

In fact, cold water swimmers from the group Outdoor Swimmer have found that cold water swimming in the winter can have a much more profound effect on mood. Those suffering with anxiety and depression have found themselves looking forward to a temperature drop in the winter, as the colder the water, the better their mental health after their wild swimming. So, this shows how natural wild swimming is and how things like changes in the weather and seasons can give stronger results on vagus nerve stimulation and resulting mental health benefits.

Is It for Everyone?

As with most holistic approaches to mental health, it's very much a trial and error approach to find exactly what works for you. Although, for many people cold water therapy is held up as a natural and effective method for combatting anxiety, depression, and trauma, it doesn't always work for everyone and its need for consistency and repeated exposure can be a struggle for some people.

One of the drawbacks of cold water therapy, which ironically is also the active ingredient in what makes it work so well, is the fact that it is all about activating that fight or flight response. This works well as, in the long term, it trains the body to handle stress more effectively and controls when the body activates that response, and in the short term, provides relief and distraction from anxiety and stress triggers. However, activating the fight or flight response can be troublesome as it exacerbates the stress and anxiety that you may be feeling, and the symptoms essentially have to get worse before they can get better. Note that when starting out with cold water therapy, panic attacks can be triggered, making the symptoms of mental health disorders worse in the short term.

But with cold water therapy, the studies show that it does work to treat mental health disorders. So, if you're able to handle the shock that comes along with starting this therapy, and are willing to consistently use the exposure, it has been proven that it will work towards training your body to deal with stress and anxiety much better than before.

Chapter 5:

Other Uses of and Treatments for the Vagus Nerve

Stimulation of the vagus nerve is not only useful in treating depression, anxiety, and trauma. This nerve is the longest nerve in the body, which means that it encompasses a wide range of organs and systems. So, it makes sense that it is responsible for, and can be detrimental to many aspects of a person's health when not functioning as it should. This section of the book details other health conditions which can deteriorate when a person's vagus nerve is not functioning properly. Many health conditions can simply be treated by the stimulation or blocking of vagus nerve function.

Furthermore, many physical health conditions can have an affect on a person's anxiety and depression when these mental health disorders are already present, or may even trigger the start of mental health problems not suffered previously. Therefore, it can be said that using the vagus nerve to treat these other health conditions could also have a positive impact on treating anxiety, depression, and trauma.

Obesity

How Is It Related to the Vagus Nerve?

Obesity can be attributed to the vagus nerve due to the nerve's connection between the digestive and esophageal systems with the brain. The vagus nerve is responsible for regulating appetite, both from its role in gut physiology and also in communication with the immune system, which affects appetite. The vagus nerve's communication structure is the reason why, when you're feeling unwell, your appetite can suffer, as it is the connecting nerve between the two systems in the body.

The vagal nerve also plays a part in the regulation of food intake, as when the intestine is stretched, signals are sent via the vagus nerve to the brain to switch off appetite. Therefore, when you feel full, it isn't necessarily because you've got a full stomach, but rather a stretched intestine. In fact, when studying mice, it was found that simulating stomach stretch, and therefore "fullness," had no effect on the mice as they continued to eat. In contrast, when they simulated intestinal stretch, it had a more profound effect on appetite and stopping the mice from eating (Intestinal Stretch Tells Brain to Switch Off Appetite, 2019). This shows how the vagus nerve is responsible for the feelings of fullness and the regulation of food intake.

Since the vagus nerve is intrinsically linked with appetite suppression and also with the sensors that indicate a feeling of fullness, it makes sense that obesity can be linked to a non-functional vagus nerve. If the vagus nerve isn't working efficiently , then messages won't be sent to the brain to let it know about fullness or intestine stretching. Plus, factors affecting appetite will also not be communicated, so appetite will constantly be activated. If a person consistently has an increased appetite and doesn't feel full, it can be assumed that they will gain weight from excess eating, leading to obesity.

Furthermore, in terms of treating obesity, as a non-functioning vagus nerve is related to a high appetite and excess eating, a stimulated vagus nerve could lead to a decreased appetite and weight loss. In an experiment by Jamie S Bodenlos (2014), chronic intermittent vagus nerve stimulation (VNS) in dogs led to an increase in weight loss across the board. The dogs that were attached to the VNS devices stopped eating much sooner than those in the control group and they also ate much less than they had previously. In humans, the results were less consistent, but 62% of those studied reported overall significant weight loss "with a quarter losing more than 5% of their body weight" (Bodenlos et al., 2014) when being treated for epilepsy using VNS.

Treating Obesity

Stimulation, or use of the vagus nerve, has been studied in many treatments for obesity. This nerve has a lot of untapped potential in the field of appetite suppression and simulating feelings of fullness, which could be life changing for those struggling with obesity.

Relaxation

The vagus nerve is responsible for many conditions that lead to obesity. Examples of this include IBS, where the body's digestive system isn't working properly so that food isn't absorbed, leading to constipation and bloating, overeating, where a hormone called ghrelin stimulates appetite by turning off the vagus nerve, and inflammation, where those with higher vagal activity have lower levels of inflammation, which is a key marker for obesity.

In this book, we have discussed many natural methods of stimulating the vagus nerve, which all boil down to relaxation. Yoga, mediation, and ASMR all increase vagal activity and vagal tone, which allows the vagus nerve to work all at full capacity decreasing appetite and properly informing the brain when a person is full.

When a person is suffering from anxiety, depression, and trauma, they can turn to comfort eating to deal with what is going on in their head. This could be due to the vagus nerve not telling the brain to decrease their appetite, so this comfort eating could turn into over eating. This overeating over a sustained period of time when mental health issues are not being treated can lead to obesity in the long term.

Most functions in the body are interconnected, and both of these issues are connected via the vagus nerve, so it's understandable that when one issue is successfully treated, the other will improve also. The better a person's mental health, the better equipped they are to battle their obesity and vice versa. When a person makes changes that reduce their obesity, this can stimulate positive changes in their mental health.

Vagus Nerve Blocking

A medical way to stimulate the vagus nerve to treat obesity is with VBLOC vagal blocking therapy (Gonzalez-Campoy MD, PhD, FACE, 2015). This is a device which works by intermittently sending electrical pulses through the abdominal vagus nerve trunk, which works to block the abdominal vagus nerve. The device is controlled by the patient's physician who decides how often and when to send the impulses to control appetite, alongside a tailored meal plan and exercise regime. This treatment shows how physical stimulation of the vagus nerve can have a positive effect on obesity, which can also be a trigger for anxiety and depression; therefore, this therapy would also have a positive effect on mental health issues.

Bariatric Surgery

A surgical option for obesity sufferers can be bariatric surgery, such as a gastric bypass. In this surgery, the small intestine is attached to the top part of the stomach, essentially making the stomach smaller and forcing food to reach the intestines much faster than it normally would. This leads to intestinal stretch which sends messages through the vagus nerve to the brain that the person is full. This means that the vagus nerve is stimulated to send these messages much earlier than it would usually, leading to quicker feelings of fullness so that less food is consumed and weight loss is promoted.

Seizures and Epilepsy

Epilepsy is a disorder where a person suffers seizures. This can start at any age and can continue for a person's entire life, although for some people, it can go away in later life. These seizures are caused by a sudden burst of electrical energy in the brain which disrupts the way that the brain functions. Messages going to and from the brain get confused and scrambled, which can then lead to a seizure. A person's seizures are generally unique to them and can range from staying alert while being stiff and still, to losing awareness and falling on the ground and jerking. Whatever the type, epilepsy and seizures are a very serious disorder which can completely disrupt a person's quality of life.

How Is It Related to the Vagus Nerve?

Although many studies have been done, no one is entirely sure what causes the unusual brain activity which leads to seizures and epilepsy. However, they can be linked to the vagus nerve because it provides the longest pathway straight to the brain. Scientists speculate that stimulating this nerve can disrupt the unusual brain activity which causes the seizures. It is also thought that the stimulation of this nerve releases chemicals in the brain that work to reduce seizures.

Treating Epilepsy

A very helpful use of the vagus nerve is in treating patients who suffer with epilepsy and seizures. Although research has shown that vagus nerve stimulation helps to treat patients with a reduction in seizures by 36% after 6 months, 58% after 4 years, and 75% by 10 years, it isn't known exactly how the treatment does this. This treatment is generally used on patients who do not respond to other medical treatments for epilepsy.

Research has shown that this treatment might be helping by stimulating the vagus nerve to increase blood flow to key brain areas that raises the levels of neurotransmitters which are important in reducing and controlling seizures. It is also thought that VNS changes EEG (electroencephalogram) patterns during a seizure. Another idea is that the majority of patients with epilepsy experience an increase in heart rate immediately before a seizure, and as discussed earlier, VNS can help to relax patients to reduce their heart rates which is helpful with reducing seizures.

Vagal Nerve Stimulation

VNS for epilepsy works by attacking a wire to the vagus nerve through the neck and implanting a device under the skin of the chest. This device sends regular, weak pulses of electrical energy into the vagus nerve, which sends the pulses to the brain. The patient is completely unaware while this is happening and has little to no side effects, other than a reduction in seizures. If a patient experiences a seizure while on a VNS device, the person can wave a magnet over the area where the device is implanted, which will send an extra pulse of stimulation to the brain. This can sometimes stop seizures in their tracks.

Arthritis

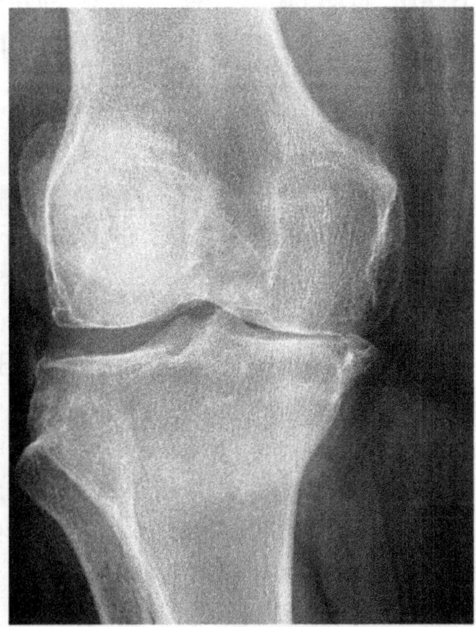

Arthritis is a condition that causes inflammation and pain in joints, like the wrist, hip or knee. It can be more prevalent in old age, but can affect anyone at any age, from young children to middle aged people.

Osteoarthritis is the most common form of arthritis that affects people above the age of 40, although can occur at any time due to injury, family history, and genetics. It affects the soft cartilage in the joints, leading to pain and discomfort. Over time, the cartilage wears away exposing the bone which leads to swelling and the production of spiny bone fragments called osteophytes. Bone will then rub on bone leading to further erosion and the possibility of bones coming out of place.

The next most common form of arthritis is rheumatoid arthritis. This affects more women than men and overall affects people over the age of 40. This condition begins if the body's immune system begins to attack and break down the joints, which leads to pain and swelling. The joints begins to change shape and then bone and cartilage begin to break down.

Arthritis is a life-changing condition that can seriously reduce someone's quality of life, as the pain stops them from being able to use their joints in the same way that they used to. Treatments for this condition range from special gloves and joint grips to joint replacements. Joints can be replaced with ceramic parts or resurfaced to replace the cartilage that has been eroded.

How Is Arthritis Related to the Vagus Nerve?

Rheumatoid arthritis is an inflammatory disorder which occurs when the body's immune system attacks the joints. Inflammation occurs when the body fights foreign bodies and injuries and tries to heal itself. The vagus nerve coordinates this as it works as the communication pathway between many organs and systems to the brain, so when the vagus nerve is triggered by injury or pain, such as rheumatoid arthritis symptoms, it sends messages to the brain that it needs to break down whatever is causing this illness in the joints.

However, this is where an issue occurs, as there is nothing in the joints that actually need breaking down, so inflammatory responses start to break down the healthy tissue in the joints. This breakdown leads to the pain and discomfort of arthritis. Since the vagus nerve is the nerve that facilitates and sends these messages which result in a wrongful inflammatory response, it makes sense that the vagus nerve is the place to start when looking to treat rheumatoid arthritis.

Treating Arthritis

When looking at the treatment of rheumatoid arthritis, it's best to go to the inflammation which causes the breakdown of the joints. Although it isn't known exactly what causes the body's autoimmune system to breakdown healthy tissue, as the vagus nerve is the system which transports the messages from the brain to the tissue, interrupting this function can be a good way to reduce the effects of arthritis.

Natural Methods

There are many holistic and natural methods of stimulating the vagus nerve, as mentioned earlier in this book. The best way to do this to treat rheumatoid arthritis is to use techniques that send strong shockwaves down the vagus nerve, as this can interrupt the messages telling the inflammatory response to attack the healthy tissue.

Cold water therapy is an effective method of shocking the vagus nerve into rebooting the parasympathetic nervous system. The cold water also leads to vasoconstriction, which can reduce swelling in the joints aiding with a reduction of pain and discomfort. This also blocks the release of the hormone histerine through the constricted blood vessels, which is the hormone that causes the feeling of pain.

Vagal Nerve Stimulation

Studies have shown that sending electrical impulses down the vagus nerve can interrupt the impulses telling the brain to attack healthy tissue with an autoimmune response. This can be done by implanting a neurostimulator called a microregulator. This microregulator stimulates the vagus nerve once a day using electrical impulses.

Data has shown that microregulators reduce systemic inflammation, and as a result, went a long way to reducing pain and disease activity in patients who were treatment resistant for rheumatoid arthritis. It was actually found that one minute of electrical stimulation per day was the most effective method of reducing symptoms of rheumatoid arthritis, even over those studied with four minutes of stimulation per day.

Chapter 6:

Vagal Nerve Stimulator

This book has been primarily concerned with informing you of the natural and holistic methods of vagus nerve stimulation used to take control of the symptoms of anxiety, depression, or trauma. But as mentioned in the previous chapter, there are methods in use which are considered to be non-natural methods of vagus nerve stimulation used to treat illnesses and ailments, which can be harnessed and repurposed for treating symptoms and eradicating mental health disorgers.

What Is a Vagal Nerve Stimulator?

The Basics

A vagal nerve stimulator is an anticonvulsant device or pulse generator. For example, a VNS device is surgically implanted into a patient's chest, which utilizes electrodes running through the patient's neck directly into their vagus nerve. This is done by exposing the carotid artery and jugular vein and coiling the electrodes around them, to provide the most effective means of sending shocks down the vagus nerve.

This device sends regular electrical impulses down the vagus nerve, stimulating the nerve. These impulses cannot be felt by the patient. The man made electrical impulses aim to scramble the impulses that are causing the body to function in an unwanted manner; for example, producing symptoms of epilepsy or depression. The aim of this therapy is to calm the irregular impulses caused by these medical disorders so that the patient can live a healthier and more balanced life.

The History

VNS therapy was originally developed for the treatment of epilepsy and seizures. The first implant of a vagus nerve stimulating device was seen in 1988, 9 years before it was approved for use as a treatment for epilepsy. The use of VNS devices was piloted and increased in frequency of use over the next few years, which showed in a number of studies a 50% decrease in seizures and overall high vagal stimulation.

As VNS therapy increased in its use in patients with epilepsy, an interesting trend emerged. It turned out that in those patients who had both epilepsy and depression and were treated with VNS, those patients showed a clinical improvement in their depressive symptoms and long term suffering of chronic depressive disorder. This trend occurred entirely unrelated to whether or not the VNS had any lasting effect on the patients' epilepsy.

From here, VNS was trialled for its use in treating treatment-resistant major depressive disorder. A trial by Rush showed that when treated with VNS, 40% to 50% of sufferers of major depressive disorders showed marked improvement in their condition. This led to the treatment being approved in the USA for its use in treating MDD. Even better, a review of the treatment in 2010 showed that over 50% showed a response to the treatment of their major depressive disorder, and 38.9% of patients went into remission for the disorder.

Today, VNS therapy is still used in treating major depressive disorder; however, it has been proven that relapses are common if device use stops. This shows how vagal tone is a constant work in progress and when someone is genetically predisposed to having low vagal tone, consistent stimulation of the vagus nerve is the best thing for treating mental health issues and keeping them at bay.

How Does It Help With Depression?

When a patient is suffering with major depressive disorder, although the exact mechanisms for causing the mental illness are unknown, it can be seen that the patient has an inadequate or changed amount of the neurotransmitters dopamine, serotonin, and norepinephrine. This tells us that there is an issue with the hormones that respond to stress and emotion. In the same way that CDD is not fully understood, the reasons why VNS therapy can improve the condition are also not completely comprehended, but scientists have a few ideas.

It's known that the vagus nerve is the "wandering" nerve and one of the places it wanders to is the area of the brain responsible for mood regulation. When a person is suffering with a chronic depressive disorder, they can feel hopeless, empty, and sad, so stimulating this area of the brain can gradually change the workings of this system to regulate moods to be more positive over time.

As we've mentioned earlier in this book, stimulating the vagus nerve can increase vagal tone which leads to a higher tolerance for stress and anxiety. Stress is an important factor in the onset and continuing relapses of chronic depressive disorder and VNS therapy is an intensive way of stimulating the vagus nerve. Therefore, as the vagus nerve is stimulated using electrical currents, the patient's vagal tone will improve and so will their response to stress, which will work to prevent an escalation or reoccurance of their CDD.

Another medical hypothesis for the cause of depression is depleted amounts of the neurotransmitters noradrenaline and 5-hydroxytryptamine. Many drugs that treat CDD work by chemically increasing the amount of NA and 5HT in the synapses; therefore, putting the brain chemicals back in balance to help treat the depression. This relates to VNS therapy because stimulating the vagus nerve using electrical currents has been proven to increase the activity of these neurotransmitters; therefore, treating the CDD by increasing their function and ability to fight against mental health disorders.

Any one of these hypotheses could be the one that is truly making a difference, or it could be a combination of all of them. But what we do know is that VNS therapy really is effective in working against the cause of chronic depressive disorder and improves the quality of life for many patients.

Other Mental Health Disorders

In this book, we have discussed the many ways in which vagus nerve stimulation can treat a range of mental health disorders. Although major depressive disorder is the first mental health disorder trialled for treatment by VNS therapy, it can be assumed that this electric current based therapy can also be effective in treating other mental health disorders which have shown positive responses to other vagus nerve stimulation.

A pilot study has shown that VNS therapy can also be useful in treating treatment-resistant anxiety disorders. In this study, a range of patients with different anxiety disorders were tested, including panic disorders, obsessive compulsive disorder, and post traumatic stress disorder. In this trial, it was shown that all patients tested showed no adverse effects from the VNS therapy and all of them tolerated it. As well, there was evidence of both short term and lasting effects in some of the patients.

Although it is in the early days of the speculation, it has been proven that stimulation of the vagus nerve can counteract the sympathetic stress response which occurs in someone with PTSD and some other anxiety disorders, by activating the parasympathetic stress response. VNS therapy can also scramble the irregular stress response to the triggers for PTSD or anxiety; therefore, helping with changing the automatic fear response when the patient is exposed to these triggers.

Is VNS for Everyone?

The short answer is no. VNS therapy, however effective, is an invasive surgical treatment that uses electrical impulses to change the function of the brain. For some people, the idea of this is both frightening and anxiety-inducing and that's completely okay. The VNS device also will leave you with scars on both your chest and neck, which isn't a significant thing when considering that it can substantially improve quality of life, but is still a consideration to be made when deciding if this is for you. You should only turn to surgical treatments like this as a last resort when every other method has failed, as this treatment is generally used on treatment-resistant patients who desperately need to improve their quality of life.

Plus, VNS can be costly if it is not covered by your insurer and locating a certified practitioner is sometimes difficult . If you're looking for a more cost effective and less invasive method of stimulating your vagus nerve to treat your mental health, this book is full of natural, holistic methods that will not break the bank. Cold water therapy, meditation, massage, and ASMR are all effective methods of improving vagal tone to decrease the effects of mental health disorders like anxiety, depression, and trauma

Conclusion

To summarise, stimulation of the vagus nerve is an effective treatment, providing long-term reduction of the symptoms of the mental health disorders of anxiety, depression, and trauma. There are many ways that you can stimulate the vagus nerve which all have their own benefits and drawbacks, with some methods being more effective for treating depression and others which are perfect for targeting chronic anxiety. In the long term, consistent use of these methods of vagal stimulation can improve overall vagal tone. This can be an effective method of keeping chronic mental health disorders at bay. Note that consistency is key, and none of the methods in this book are short-term fixes (although they do have short-term benefits) and the more that you practice these techniques, the better you will feel, and the closer you will get to saying goodbye to your mental health issues.

What is the Vagus Nerve Really For?

Among other things, the vagus nerve is concerned with the function of the mind. This nerve is the longest in the body and is responsible for functions across the cardiac, pulmonary, digestive, and esophageal systems. However, this nerve having its finger in so many metaphorical pies is precisely the defining factor which makes it so effective in treating mental health disorders.

If you have been struggling with disorders like anxiety, depression, and trauma, you will know that you suffer not only with the emotional feelings that come along with these disorders, but also physical effects like IBS, chest pain, and lethargy which can come along with them. In fact, these physical side effects can both result from and contribute to your mental health issues, creating a downwards spiral into deeper anxiety or depression.

Treating the side effects of mental health disorders through vagus nerve stimulation can make it easier to pull yourself out of the throes of unwanted symptoms, while simultaneously treating the brain chemistry responsible for them. The reason why vagus nerve stimulation is so important and effective as a mental health treatment is because it is connected to all of the systems that can help to make a person feel good or bad.

Improving Vagal Tone and Why It's Important

Vagal tone refers to the strength of your vagus nerve, and how effectively it is working to facilitate the messages being sent from the systems it connects to the brain. When a person has low vagal tone, it means that messages are not sent properly and can be missed, leading to systems not working properly; for example, hunger signals not being sent to the brain or a heightened response to fear stimuli. When a person has low vagal tone, they are more susceptible and likely to have poor mental health, and can suffer from anxiety, depression, and trauma.

It is possible to be born with low vagal tone, which can be the cause of genetic and chronic depression and anxiety. Low vagal tone can also occur when the vagus nerve doesn't get enough stimulation. Vagal tone can be improved by increased and regular stimulation of the vagus nerve. When this happens and vagal tone improves, a person will find that their mental health symptoms will improve and it will be easier to recover from chronic mental health disorders. This needs to be practiced consistently to keep vagal tone high and mental health symptoms at bay.

Natural and Holistic Methods of Stimulating Your Vagus Nerve

ASMR

Autonomous sensory meridian response, or ASMR, is a relatively new treatment for mental health disorders. This technique is unique in the way that it was developed by users of ASMR for other users. Its scientific applications and the reasoning behind the response has been actively studied in more recent years. It works by using audio and visual triggers which simulate methods of relaxation, in an attempt to invoke tingles in the viewer or listener. These tingles are not felt by everyone who participates and only people who experience ASMR tingles will find this technique to be useful. This treatment stimulates the vagus nerve by triggering a PNS response through deep breathing and relaxation and is heralded by users and ASMRtists for its uses in treating anxiety, depression, and trauma. There are even specific "cranial nerve examination" role-plays which use the science behind cranial nerves (the vagus nerve being the 10th cranial nerve) to invoke a relaxation response.

Meditation

An older and religiously significant form of vagal stimulation is meditation, which has been practiced around the world for thousands of years. This technique involves a focus on deep breathing and taking the mind off of the stresses of everyday life, which results in relaxation and relief from mental health disorders. The deep breathing triggers responses to be sent down the vagus nerve, stimulating it and giving short term relaxation and long-term improvement in vagal tone. Meditation has been used since 5000 BCE in religions such as Buddhism, Sikkhism, and Islam, but has in more recent years been studied for its benefits in treating mental health disorders and overall, promoting a sense of relaxation and calm.

Massage

Another treatment that has been used since ancient times and employs relaxation techniques to provide vagal stimulation is massage. Massage comes in many forms, but at its base level, it uses touch stimulation to relax patients with an aim of promoting an overall sense of calm. This relaxation triggers a vagal response through the lung stretch receptors, stimulating the vagus nerve and contributing to overall vagal tone. There are also other massage techniques such as reflexology that use specific pressure points, including points along the vagus nerve like the carotid artery. This gives a more direct physical massage onto the vagus nerve and provides more effective vagal stimulation. All of these techniques improve mental health by treating abnormal brain currents that pass down the vagus nerve which relaxes the systems, so that they function more normally to promote overall calm.

Cold Water Therapy

Similar to massage and meditation, forms of cold water therapy have been practiced for a very long time and their benefits have been passed down through generations. However, where they differ from other treatments discussed in this book is how they work. This type of treatment stimulates the vagus nerve by providing a big shock (the shock of freezing cold water) which can jerk the mind out of anxious or depressive patterns to provide a sort of cranial reset. This can be applied in many forms, from cold showers to wild water swimming.

Cold water therapy is extremely effective in treating depression as the shock activates the fight or flight response, which stimulates the vagus nerve massively and starts the nerve passing messages properly between systems which can be otherwise missed when a person is suffering with depression. This therapy is also useful in treating anxiety and trauma because of its vagal stimulation effects, which can improve overall vagal tone and reduce stress and anxious feelings in the body.

Which Treatment Is for You?

You might be wondering which of these techniques could be the one that works best for your mental health condition. The best way to find out would be by trial and error. All of these treatments may work for you or none of them might, but as all of these treatments at their heart use relaxation techniques, it is likely you will find some benefit from trying them out even if they don't completely cure your anxiety, depression or trauma.

Another great option is combining these methods to attack the problem from multiple sides. Try meditating in the bath or massaging your carotid artery while listening to ASMR audio, for a two-pronged approach to vagus nerve stimulation and relaxation. These techniques all have their unique benefits and the more vagus nerve stimulation you practice at any one time, the stronger will be the effect on the relaxation.

Remember that the best way to practice holistic methods of relaxation and vagal stimulation is to be consistent. You may not see massive results right away, but over time, these methods will improve your vagal tone and this will go a long way towards treating your chronic mental health issues, and the more you practice, the stronger the effects will become.

Surgical Methods of Vagal Stimulation

You have likely picked up this book as it gives insight into the natural and holistic methods of vagal stimulation which improve vagal tone and help to treat mental health issues.

However, if these do not work and your chronic problems with depression and anxiety persist, there are surgical options available that use techniques of vagal stimulation to solve these problems. This involves having a device implanted in the chest and neck, which sends electrical impulses down the vagus nerve and scramble impulses relating to depression and anxiety. This technique has been proven to be very effective in treating treatment-resistant depression and has also been trialled for anxiety.

This is not a treatment that works for everyone and we do recommend that the more natural and holistic methods laid out in this book should be tried first for their vagus nerve stimulating effects. Then, as a last resort, you could turn to surgery. Plus, even if you do find that the surgical option is the best fit for you, it is always a good idea to work on your vagal tone through holistic methods and consistently practice your mediation, ASMR, massage and/or water therapy as they can continue to make improvements in your overall mental health.

Final Thoughts

If your life has been affected by disorders such as depression, anxiety, and trauma, hopefully this book will provide some useful methods to work on your vagal tone to provide some relief from your symptoms.

These mental health disorders can have debilitating effects on a person's life and it can be very difficult to find exactly what works in terms of treatment, with doctors prescribing different pills and discussing complicated ideas that can have side effects which may make life even harder than before. If you have tried pharmaceutical methods and find that they affect your mind in ways that you don't like, or if you have discussed the idea of using surgical methods with your doctor, but find the idea frightening and overwhelming, don't worry. These are not only methods of treating mental health and shouldn't be the first things you try when tackling your anxiety or depression.

With this book, we aim to show some completely natural and holistic methods that harness the power of the vagus nerve to promote short-term relaxation and relief, while also reducing the symptoms of chronic illness.

Remember that this is a marathon and not a sprint, and if you have chronic low vagal tone, you will need to use these methods consistently to reap the benefits of having high vagal tone. The more you practice the techniques, the better you are going to feel and your life will keep getting better and better.

References

Auracle, T. (2016, August 9). *The Special Powers Series - YouTube.* Www.YouTube.Com. https://www.YouTube.com/playlist?list=PLpYIOdC2P_AUT ojWXXFix3oMKfDaS8XRS

Berzin, R. (2016, March 20). *The Nerve That Stops You From Losing Weight and Upsets Your Stomach.* Parsley Health. https://www.parsleyhealth.com/blog/vagusnerveweightloss/

Bodenlos, J. S., Schneider, K. L., Oleski, J., Gordon, K., Rothschild, A. J., & Pagoto, S. L. (2014). Vagus Nerve Stimulation and Food Intake. *Journal of Diabetes Science and Technology,* *8*(3), 590–595. https://doi.org/10.1177/1932296814525188

Bongiorno, P. (2014). *A Cold Splash–Hydrotherapy for Depression and Anxiety.* Psychology Today. https://www.psychologytoday.com/gb/blog/innersource/201407/cold-splash-hydrotherapy-depression-and-anxiety

Browning, K. N., Verheijden, S., & Boeckxstaens, G. E. (2017). The Vagus Nerve in Appetite Regulation, Mood, and Intestinal Inflammation. *Gastroenterology*, *152*(4), 730–744. https://doi.org/10.1053/j.gastro.2016.10.046

Cafasso, J. (2017, October 6). *Do Binaural Beats Have Health Benefits?* Healthline; Healthline Media. https://www.healthline.com/health/binaural-beats

Cannon, J. (2015, February 20). *The Simple Truth to Modern Meditation.* HuffPost. https://www.huffpost.com/entry/modern-meditation-a-uniqu_b_6443280

Caponigro, J. P. (2012, August 27). *All Religions Practice Forms Of Meditation.* John Paul Caponigro – Digital Photography Workshops, DVDs, EBooks. https://www.johnpaulcaponigro.com/blog/9419/all-religions-practice-forms-of-meditation-meditation-is-a-universal-practice/#:~:text=The%20five%20major%20religions%20%E2%80%93%20Hinduism

Chmelik, S. (2019, April 30). *Vagus Nerve Stimulation*. Sensate. https://www.getsensate.com/blogs/news/vagus-nerve-stimulation

Clarke, R. (2018, September 28). *Swim Positive*. Outdoorswimmer.Com. https://outdoorswimmer.com/blogs/swim-positive#:~:text=It

Cooper, B. B. (2013, August 21). *What is Meditation & How Does It Affects Our Brains? | Buffer*. Buffer Resources. https://buffer.com/resources/how-meditation-affects-your-brain/

Cresswell, J. D. (2016). Alterations in Resting-State Functional Connectivity Link Mindfulness Meditation With Reduced Interleukin-6: A Randomized Controlled Trial. *Biological Psychiatry*, *80*(1), 53–61. https://doi.org/10.1016/j.biopsych.2016.01.008

European League Against Rheumatism. (2019, June 14). *Vagus nerve stimulation study shows significant reduction in rheumatoid arthritis symptoms: Initial pilot data support the use of new neurostimulation treatment in a larger study in patients who have failed current standard of care.* ScienceDaily. https://www.sciencedaily.com/releases/2019/06/1906140829 31.htm

Field, T. (2010). Pregnancy and labor massage. *Expert Review of Obstetrics & Gynecology, 5*(2), 177–181. https://doi.org/10.1586/eog.10.12

Furness, P. (2020, April 20). *VAGUS NERVE.* MAX Remedial Massage and Therapy. https://maxremedial.com/blog/hyntwmh8l7ynb5gx4zgsgjsla5 nrhy

Gonzalez-Campoy MD, PhD, FACE, J. M. (2015, March 15). *Newly Approved Weight Loss Device Blocks the Vagus Nerve.* EndocrineWeb.

https://www.endocrineweb.com/professional/obesity/newly-approved-weight-loss-device-blocks-vagus-nerve

Gottfried, S. (2017, March 8). *Viva Las Vagus: How Vagal Tone Impacts Your Health (and 10 Ways to Improve It)*. Www.Saragottfriedmd.Com. https://www.saragottfriedmd.com/viva-las-vagus-how-vagal-tone-impacts-your-health-and-10-ways-to-%E2%80%8Eimprove-it%E2%80%8E/

Hudson, V. (2015, September 7). *Cold water bathing — a Victorian craze that really is good for your health*. Spectator Life. https://life.spectator.co.uk/articles/cold-water-bathing-was-a-victorian-craze-but-it-really-is-good-for-your-health/#:~:text=The%20practice%20of%20medically%20sanctioned

Intestinal Stretch Tells Brain to Switch Off Appetite. (2019, November 15). GEN - Genetic Engineering and Biotechnology News. https://www.genengnews.com/news/intestinal-stretch-tells-brain-to-switch-off-appetite/

Jamie Lauren Keiles. (2019, April 4). How A.S.M.R. Became a Sensation. *The New York Times.* https://www.nytimes.com/2019/04/04/magazine/how-asmr-videos-became-a-sensation-YouTube.html

Jungmann, M., Vencatachellum, S., Van Ryckeghem, D., & Vögele, C. (2018). Effects of Cold Stimulation on Cardiac-Vagal Activation in Healthy Participants: Randomized Controlled Trial. *JMIR Formative Research, 2*(2). https://doi.org/10.2196/10257

Kok, B. E., & Fredrickson, B. L. (2010). Upward spirals of the heart: Autonomic flexibility, as indexed by vagal tone, reciprocally and prospectively predicts positive emotions and social connectedness. *Biological Psychology, 85*(3), 432–436. https://doi.org/10.1016/j.biopsycho.2010.09.005

Lee, M., Song, C.-B., Shin, G.-H., & Lee, S.-W. (2019). Possible Effect of Binaural Beat Combined With Autonomous Sensory Meridian Response for Inducing Sleep. *Frontiers in Human Neuroscience, 13.* https://doi.org/10.3389/fnhum.2019.00425

Lopez, G. (2015, July 15). *ASMR, explained: why YouTube videos of people whispering are so popular.* Vox; Vox. https://www.vox.com/2015/7/15/8965393/asmr-video-YouTube-autonomous-sensory-meridian-response

Luchau, T. (2017, December). *Working with the Vagus Nerve.* Www.Abmp.Com. https://www.abmp.com/textonlymags/article.php?article=1777#:~:text=The%20Vagus%20Nerve%20Technique

McIntyre, C. K. (2018). Is there a role for vagus nerve stimulation in the treatment of posttraumatic stress disorder? *Bioelectronics in Medicine,* *1*(2), 95–99. https://doi.org/10.2217/bem-2018-0002

Meditation for Beginners. (2020). Headspace. https://www.headspace.com/meditation/meditation-for-beginners

Miwa, H., Kondo, T., Oshima, T., Fukui, H., Tomita, T., & Watari, J. (2010). Esophageal Sensation and Esophageal Hypersensitivity - Overview From Bench to Bedside. *Journal of*

Neurogastroenterology and Motility, *16*(4), 353–362. https://doi.org/10.5056/jnm.2010.16.4.353

Nall, R. (2019, July 12). *Cold shower benefits*. Www.Medicalnewstoday.Com. https://www.medicalnewstoday.com/articles/325725#stronger-immune-system

Ogbonnaya, S., & Kaliaperumal, C. (2013). Vagal nerve stimulator: Evolving trends. *Journal of Natural Science, Biology, and Medicine*, *4*(1), 8–13. https://doi.org/10.4103/0976-9668.107254

Pritchard, E. (2019, January 3). *ASMR: The Mind-Soothing Trend Dominating Your Feed*. Women's Health. https://www.womenshealthmag.com/uk/health/sleep/a25613360/asmr/

Rosenberg, S. (2019). *ACCESSING THE HEALING POWER OF THE VAGUS NERVE : self-exercises for anxiety, depression, trauma,... and autism*. Readhowyouwant Com Ltd.

Ross, A. (2016, March 9). *How Meditation Went Mainstream.* Time; Time. https://time.com/4246928/meditation-history-buddhism/

Schultz, R. (2018, September 5). *Relieve anxiety in 10 seconds.* Furthermore from Equinox. https://furthermore.equinox.com/articles/2018/05/anxiety-reducing-hand-massage

Sherman, K. J., Ludman, E. J., Cook, A. J., Hawkes, R. J., Roy-Byrne, P. P., Bentley, S., Brooks, M. Z., & Cherkin, D. C. (2010). Effectiveness of therapeutic massage for generalized anxiety disorder: a randomized controlled trial. *Depression and Anxiety, 27*(5), 441–450. https://doi.org/10.1002/da.20671

Shevchuk, N. A. (2008). Adapted cold shower as a potential treatment for depression. *Medical Hypotheses, 70*(5), 995–1001. https://doi.org/10.1016/j.mehy.2007.04.052

Siems, W. G., van Kuijk, F. J. G. M., Maass, R., & Brenke, R. (1994). Uric acid and glutathione levels during short-term whole body cold exposure. *Free Radical Biology and Medicine,*

16(3), 299–305. https://doi.org/10.1016/0891-5849(94)90030-2

Stanborough, R. J. (2020, July 8). *What to Know About Cold Water Therapy.* Healthline; Healthline Media. https://www.healthline.com/health/cold-water-therapy#benefits

Team Lemonade. (2019, March 14). *This Is Why Oddly Satisfying Videos Are Trending.* Lemonade Blog. https://www.lemonade.com/blog/oddly-satisfying-videos-instagram-reddit/

University of Sheffield. (2018, June 21). *Brain tingles: First study of its kind reveals physiological benefits of ASMR.* ScienceDaily. https://www.sciencedaily.com/releases/2018/06/180621101334.htm

Vagal Response - How to Strengthen Vagus Nerve. (2017, November 29). Dave Asprey Blog. https://blog.daveasprey.com/vagus-nerve-vagal-response/

Vagus nerve | anatomy. (2019). In *Encyclopædia Britannica*. https://www.britannica.com/science/vagus-nerve

Vagus nerve Nerve: Vagus nerve. (n.d.). https://www.caam.rice.edu/~cox/wrap/vagusnerve.pdf

WhisperingLife ASMR. (2009). Whisper 1 - hello! [YouTube Video]. In *YouTube*. https://www.YouTube.com/watch?v=IHtgPbfTgKc

Zimmerman, E. (2019, May 9). *I Now Suspect the Vagus Nerve Is the Key to Well-being*. The Cut. https://www.thecut.com/2019/05/i-now-suspect-the-vagus-nerve-is-the-key-to-well-being.html

Images

Figure 1.

Geralt. (2017). Brain nerves. In *Pixabay*. https://pixabay.com/photos/brain-biology-anatomy-think-2676370/

Figure 2.

Wokandapix. (2020). ASMR. In *Pixabay*. https://pixabay.com/photos/asmr-autonomous-sensory-meridian-4861163/

Figure 3.

USA-Reiseblogger. (2016). YouTube tablet. In *Pixabay*. https://pixabay.com/photos/YouTube-tablet-news-app-computer-1719926/

Figure 4.

12019. (2013). Optometrist. In *Pixabay*. https://pixabay.com/photos/optometrist-doctor-patient-eye-91750/

Figure 5.

Sasint. (2016). Buddhist Monk Sitting. In *Pixabay*.
https://pixabay.com/photos/buddhist-monk-sitting-
meditation-1807526/

Figure 6.

Lograstudio. (2018). Yoga exercise fitness. In *Pixabay*.
https://pixabay.com/photos/yoga-exercise-fitness-woman-
health-3053488/

Figure 7.

andreas160578. (2016). Treatment finger. In *Pixabay*.
https://pixabay.com/photos/treatment-finger-keep-hand-
wrist-1327811/

Figure 8.

Loseitlady. (2013). England United Kingdom Bath. In *Pixabay*.
https://pixabay.com/photos/england-united-kingdom-bath-
170402/

Figure 9.

Edmonds, A. (2017). Open Water Swim. In *Pixabay*. https://pixabay.com/photos/open-water-swim-mass-swim-ironman-2696689/

Figure 10.

Taokinesis. (2020). Knee Xray. In *Pixabay*. https://pixabay.com/photos/knee-x-rays-arthritis-skeleton-5314881/